No They Persisted

Gaining Emotional Intelligence in the Wake of Adult Child Estrangement

CHRISTINE PARSONS

outskirts press

Nevertheless They Persisted
Gaining Emotional Intelligence in the Wake of Adult Child Estrangement
All Rights Reserved.
Copyright © 2023 Christine Parsons
v2.0

The opinions expressed in this manuscript are solely the opinions of the author and do not represent the opinions or thoughts of the publisher. The author has represented and warranted full ownership and/or legal right to publish all the materials in this book.

This book may not be reproduced, transmitted, or stored in whole or in part by any means, including graphic, electronic, or mechanical without the express written consent of the publisher except in the case of brief quotations embodied in critical articles and reviews.

Outskirts Press, Inc.
http://www.outskirtspress.com

ISBN: 978-1-9772-5292-0

Cover Photo © 2023 Christie C. Girouard. All rights reserved - used with permission.

Outskirts Press and the "OP" logo are trademarks belonging to Outskirts Press, Inc.

PRINTED IN THE UNITED STATES OF AMERICA

I would like to express my gratitude and appreciation for my friends, Ariella Neville, and Jeffrey Simpson who assisted me in creating some very special images.

Dedication

(Christine Parsons Photo)

To my posse: I am forever grateful for all your love and support as I walk this path unchosen. There is great challenge in rewriting what we believed to be true. Committing to this process requires a community who freely bestows the gift of empathy.

(Ariella Neville Photo)

To my husband and son: thank you for standing by me every time I fall apart. I recognize the silent strength it takes to resist trying to fix me. Your faith has always given me the courage to put myself back together.

Table of Contents

Preface i
Introduction: Journey of a Mother's Heart vii
Author's Note xiii
The Repetitive Power 1
They Want Crazy...Don't Give Them Crazy 6
Movement 14
Birth Days.. 18
Gather Your Posse 21
The Ripple Effect 25
Freya 27
Mother's Day 31
How to Fix Estrangement 35
When It Becomes Necessary to Distance
with Love 38
Reconciliation 42
Set Up to Fail 45
Grieving 52
Christmas 56
Historical Hysteria 59
Weathering the Tide 62
My Feelings About Regret 64
Holding On 66
Muddled in Confusion 69
Finding Solid Ground 72
Grandparent Alienation 76
Letter to My Grandchildren 81

Not Enough	83
The Anatomy of Estrangement	86
Move On and Let Go	88
Emotional Strategy	91
Unto Us? Or to Themselves?	94
Common Denominator?	97
Hit From Behind	99
Saved From Drowning	101
Stirring the Pot	103
Imagine	106
When the Mourning Doesn't End	109
To Peanut	111
Grandchildren	113
Who Holds Your Hand?	115
Tears That Cleanse	117
To Be Seen for Who You Are	119
Walking a Path Unchosen	122
Tell the Universe	125
Don't Take the Bait	127
No Matter Where You Go, You Bring Yourself	130
When Expectation Finds Reality	132
I Grieve	133
The Estranged Parent and Alienated Grandparent Often Feel They Are Walking... The Yellow Brick Road	135
Preserving the Open Wound	137
Save Yourself	140
Desperation	143
The Muddy Puddle	145

Change	148
Shoulda, Woulda, Coulda	151
Day of the Robe	152
Be Your Own Definition	154
Are You Here for Good?	155
Be the Light	158
Solutions?	161
Free Will	163
Morning Means Mourning	166
Be Part of Your Own Story	169
Never Beg for Crumbs	172
How Is Today?	178
DNA	181
Can Your Adult Child Forget You?	184
Fragmentation	187
Answers?	191
You	194
What We Believe as True	198
Planning	200
Gaslighting	202
A Wedding	205
The Cause-the Cure-the Control	208
Does the Punishment Fit the Crime?	212
Letter from My Daughter 2001	216
How It Fades....	219
Introduction to a Private Support Group	222
Emotional Paralysis	226
When the Implication Is Your Wrong Doing	228
Thanksgiving	230

Choices	236
Holidaze	240
Letters of Amends?	243
If My Daughters Were Listening	247
When Left Unspoken	250
The Value of a Sincere Apology	254
Getting What You Deserve?	256
Would You Do It Again?	260
Epilogue	264

Preface

OUR HUMAN INTERACTIONS are fragile. Things are great, as long as they are great. Family is everything when we are everything to family. But the minute we stumble over a breakdown in communication, what seems an impenetrable bond can suddenly be fractured. This weakness creates a vulnerability, and we get overly emotional. Fighting for what we believe is true.

Our life experience teaches us to make choices based on what we know. If provoked by unresolved conflict, these decisions might evolve with lesser logic. Being in a relationship with someone who struggles with their past, might find an unsettled future. If you have known this person for years, there is a tendency to see them for who you want them to be. This is true of all relationships, even with our own adult children. And so, I have adopted a philosophy around this: concentrate on the relationships that offer quality not quantity. When there are both, it is a blessing.

This is the third time I have experienced estrangement from my daughters. A truth I didn't think I could survive. I felt surrounded by darkness. The pain was so great I prayed for my premature end. The accusations of failure as a mother and a human seemed a burden I could not carry.

My community began to worry that my fall down the rabbit hole had no bottom. They watched me plummet head first toward my belief of being powerless. But if someone says you are a failure, does that make it true?

Though my writing is based on Adult Child Estrangement, I have found that it fits in all the places where we cannot impose our will. Decisions are based on what we know, but also where we place the most value. A difficult reality when someone you love chooses to live as if you don't exist.

I wasn't being seen for who I am. There were countless times that I was told I need to be different. An interesting paradox that offered me a constant state of confusion. No matter how hard I tried to fit into their mold, I was either too big or too small. There was always something wrong. A friend said to me, "They just want you to be pastel. But you are a woman of bright and vivid color." I have found great peace in her perception. When all is said and done, I want to look back on my life as being authentically me. To avoid the ill-fated journey of living according to someone else's expectations.

My changed perspective finds that the pursuit of happiness is a destination. Once there, we are already in search of the next thing. My choice is to live in joy. This creates a lifestyle and a mindset. To reside in this space, lends an opportunity to celebrate the life we have been given, while acknowledging the life we thought we would have.

Recovery is the desire to heal from within. Those feelings of emotional conflict provoke a decision. Do we want to hold on? Or release the grip? Everyone has memories they wish to reconstruct, but there are no do-overs. It is worth the effort to heal past trauma, allowing these experiences to become part of who you are. We are best when we live inside our reality. Denying the truth takes a lot of energy that can be used for a greater purpose.

As an estranged mother, I did grasp for literature that implied I could "fix" my daughters. There are many books written on conflict resolution with adult children. But the key to this is a willingness to engage and seek the truth. What happens when silence is the answer? What happens when you must come to terms with the unimaginable truth? Soaking in a reality that your beautiful adult child does not want this to get better.

As the years have rolled past, there have been many light bulb moments. A more concrete definition of what it is to control people, places, and things. I have learned that there is no such thing. Yet friends will continue to imply that you can overpower other people's thoughts. They will make suggestions that there is a simple solution to things so complex. An implication that you can commandeer your child's behavior. Sometimes feigning the reality of zero contact, "Well, that's ridiculous." And perhaps continue by stating the obvious: "You are the parent." And the conclusion: "They can't just stop talking to you." Or, "They'll come around. They just need to mature."

At this point, these offerings, though well intended, seem silly. Adult Child Estrangement is a path riddled with doubt and uncertainty. When you read any story of reconciliation, it resembles someone who has been deprived of food and water. You slurp and devour every word, believing that there are people out there who have finally found the key to this impenetrable force. But this is not a journey of one size fits all. When the people are different, so are the solutions. As much as we want to move forward, we can't force others to take our hand. There has to be a desire from everyone to listen and engage. The reality of confronting contrary beliefs can be like trying to push rope uphill. Independent thinking creates free will, which is difficult to capture.

In the meantime, each sunrise is filled with a need for empathy. Morning means mourning. Blinking our eyes open, only to remember the day ahead will push us to be brave. We begin to step away from people who have misguided expectations. Friends who think we can simply move on, let go, stop crying, or just forget can add to the burden of all things impossible.

Please, see me for who I am: a tender heart that mourns for her family, though still alive. Be kind to my process when there are good days and bad. There is no destination that will free me of my grief. The truth has rewritten my address book. I search for dear souls who can sit with me in my sadness. They are able to do this without offering solutions.

My repeated mantra before the silence put an end to my screaming: "What do I need to do to move us to a better place?" Only to hear more character defects which never led to an answer. Reconciliation will happen when words are spoken with the intention to heal. Until that moment, life goes on.

Believe me, I have left no stone unturned. I begged, pleaded, threw away my pride, incessantly apologized, sent gifts, texts, e-mails, and even showed up once unannounced. All to no avail. Reality was right in front of me. I was alone in my effort to create change for the better. This truth gave me clarity. My emotional work is acceptance.

At first this sounded like a shrill cry. Acceptance was abrasive to all the senses. My despair was palpable. My effort came in baby steps. I was not prepared for this journey. The map of my life was laid out before me. How on earth would I ever live peacefully given these circumstances? And then I realized that acceptance is not a destination. It is a daily mindful practice. It doesn't require me to say, "This is OK." Acceptance means you are living inside your own reality. There will still be days when the truth hurts too much.

Time has given me the courage to embrace the moments when I have arrived. I give myself compassion on the days that find me in a puddle. All the while, I live being authentically me. Being an estranged mother is part of who I am. But I won't let this be my entire existence. Forward motion pushes me to gain in emotional intelligence.

I reflect on the chaos and understand that there was never a right answer. Unconditional love does not require a defense. I am at my best when I involve myself with people who don't need to be convinced. They greet me with sincerity, and put all judgement aside. These are the dear souls who give me the courage to fix myself when I feel broken. No one can do this for us. Other people don't have power over the way we feel. So, when I find myself in times of struggle, I turn to those who easily bestow the gift of empathy. This lies within simple, yet powerful words: "How is today?" which allows me to be honest; "This must hurt so much." Acknowledges that my grief is ongoing.

Gather your posse and circle the wagons.

Introduction: Journey of a Mother's Heart

(Christine Parsons Family Album)

THERE IS A special and distinct place in a parent's heart—a compartment that grows when our children are placed in our arms for the very first time. I was given the opportunity to explore this place inside me. I have been blessed with experience and a discovery of strength that would not be known, if not for the path I have taken. I am able to retrace every footstep in the sand. I find the salt of my tears sweet. My joy is immeasurable, just for the knowing of despair.

A deafening silence fell between me and my daughter. Words were spoken, yet resounded foreign and indecipherable. Each of us had our own code for pain, lost to one another's interpretation. Scrambles of words, emotions, tears, and frustration. Puzzles of pieces that didn't fit. A deepening pit into darkness that grew with each encounter. And we spiraled and fell without wings.

I don't remember the exact moment that I felt my daughter no longer loved me. I had believed from conception that biology held a cosmic connection. A life born inside my womb would continue to flourish in open air, always in sight—a love that never reached farther than the length of a mother's arms.

The dance of estrangement between mother and child is mysterious and off beat. It is uncoordinated and disconnected. It threatens the nervous system and challenges perception. A mother stomping furiously and frantically to find solid ground realizes her fragility of power. The terrifying reality creeps in. Control beyond our own thoughts and actions does not exist. A paralyzing grip takes hold when you know that sight must become inward and not toward horizons.

I fell to earth. My nightmares allowed me to hit the ground. Most wake up seconds before. I became the only person on the planet. Feelings of isolation, self-doubt, and guilt imprisoned me. I was terrified all the time. I lived for months of tomorrows without reaping the glory of moments. I hit bottom when I found myself face down on hands and knees, searching for lies.

The truth finds its way, whether we want to know it or not. We are given insight to our power for choice. The truth presents us with tremendous opportunity to rejoice in life's simplicity. Moments of grandeur come few and far between, while the little things constantly surround us. There is glory in seeing the forest for the trees. It is empowering to capture the journey as a whole and not a specific moment, and therefore, accepting that today is our reality. Tomorrow will never come in less than twenty-four hours.

The honesty of hope and fibers of strength burst from that compartment in my heart. With me or apart from me, I know my love for my daughter. She would always be born of my body and carried with me each and every day. I gracefully bow to the process of distancing with love. For a mother, it bears a semblance of giving up—initially riddled with uncertainty, and then, mercifully, it gives way to recognition. We are powerless to make choices for others. Even for our own children.

I wrote this during my first (six year) estrangement with my youngest daughter. So many words remain unspoken. I flew to her in Africa, during her time with the Peace Corps. My hope was that this far and distant continent had the power to heal our wounds. I believed that my effort to bridge oceans would allow us to begin anew. Perhaps we could leave our painful past behind. Together, we might gain the strength and courage needed to override the conflict of our blended family.

Those two weeks were the most amazing fourteen days in the history of our mother-daughter relationship. She was twenty-five and I felt, for the first time, that she really liked me. There was a sense of pride when she introduced me as her mom. Our time together passed seamlessly, and I flew home filled with hope.

There were five months that followed. They were rich with fully engaged phone calls and text messages. But when she returned home, to US soil, the conflict arrived with her. Once back to the bosom of truth, our blended family dynamics took their place. Our horrible circumstances started all over again. It was with such intensity; it was as if Africa had never happened.

The first estrangement just led to the next, and then the next. I can see clearly now that unresolved conflict has a deep and repetitive power. It gets worse each time. Those traumas of the past require a conversation. There are chapters in our story that beg to be reconciled. Without a dialogue meant to heal, the past will keep showing up. There is no pretending that bad things never happened. It will only create a path lined with eggshells. No matter how hard we try to tip toe, the fragile layers still break beneath our feet.

The conflict left unspoken evolves into a big fat elephant. It sits comfortably in the middle of the living room. The question that begs for answers: "How did you get in here? What do we need to do to get you to leave once and for all?"

Our inability to put the unrest into words has created a tornado that devasted our family. There was no way to stop the destruction. In 2016, both of my daughters would render me silent. It is the unimaginable. But life goes on....

Author's Note

THE FOLLOWING EXCERPTS are articles representative of how I was feeling on a particular day. A diary of sorts that evolves with emotion. Perhaps you might read straight through, or maybe you will use my experiences as reference on days when the struggle feels insurmountable. There are certain expressions that will be read as repetitious. There are days when I go to my own words for reminders. I admit that my insecurities riddle me with fear. Every day is met with the question, "Am I on the right path?" My intention is to give my pain a purpose. To evolve with compassion, in knowing my adult children are struggling with their own truth. It is work to free one's self from anger and expectation.

As my journey unfolds, I have gained an increasing awareness. Estranged parents have those days when they feel they have been forgotten. But then I think of the specific energy it takes to remain silent. Our estranged children must show up every day to renew their anger. All those emotions to target the one person who was there no matter what. When anger prevails, the turmoil remains. We can only come to irreconcilable differences, through the effort of reconciling. Breathless and exhausted from the search for peaceful solutions. With silence in its place, all the things that went wrong stay wrong.

I poured my soul into this book. My hope is that I can offer other estranged parents a perspective on their own feelings as well as others. I have experienced those moments of desperation. Seemingly dropped off on a desert island with no supplies. Screaming, but no one can hear. Ashamed of being banished to a place where no one can find me. And if they do, the sound of my voice comes out like a whisper: "I was put here because my own children want nothing to do with me." The helicopter immediately takes flight without me, and the overwhelming loneliness returns. This is how I felt for a stretch of many days.

Estrangement provokes a self-deprecating inner dialogue. It is a journey riddled with guilt, shame, and judgement. In order to save myself, I had to "come out" and own this experience. And so, I speak out loud without fear of repercussion. The worst has already happened. My life must evolve around that truth.

When we walk a path unchosen, it is vital to find purpose and gain a sense of direction. This experience, for me, has resulted in the growth of my emotional intelligence. I was once told that talking about feelings is my greatest weakness. Today, I know it is my super power.

I wish you, and your tender hearts, peace as you continue your forward march. You are here with a purpose, and you are never alone.

The Repetitive Power

(Christine Parsons Family Album)

IN 2007, MY youngest daughter entered The Peace Corps. Though she lived across town with the father, she left that September without saying goodbye. I remember falling to my knees the day she was to board the first plane toward Africa. I had to face the horrible reality that she would be gone for the next twenty-seven months.

For over a year, I would get unsolicited information, "Tiegan is doing so well." Or, I saw Alice (step-mom) in the post office mailing your daughter a huge care package." These offerings resounded inside my head like a bull horn. It is the most crippling experience to receive news of your own child through other people.

My eldest daughter's engagement and pending marriage was a catalyst to how deeply fragmented we had become. I had this vision of our broken family needing distance during a milestone celebration. A wedding reception with a line drawn to remain on separate sides of the room. Where to begin in effort to unite? I had my daughter's phone number in my hand, and I pressed each button with conviction. My heart was pounding inside my ears, and the call connected. "Hi Tiegan, it's Mom."

The sound of my voice came as quite a shock to her. There were many pregnant pauses as the distance of estrangement was prevalent. We grabbed hold of small talk, and slowly began a renewal of familiarity. From that day, we continued our correspondence and gained a sense of comfort. Soon thereafter, I sent her a care package of my own. I wanted her to share the experience of Halloween with her students. I enclosed the following letter:

> September 11, 2008
> Dear Tiegan,
>
> Many Septembers have passed. I reminisce with great sadness over the months, and now years that find me blacked out. I struggle a bit to find equilibrium. Today the 7th anniversary of an epic event in history. Time is precious.

Giving heart to those we love does not find a holiday. It is a constant state of being.

I find that I am judged as to the mother I have been. I continue to recall my life with children and feel a deep sense of pride. Given the chance to do it all over again, I would remain the parent that I am, and will continue to be. I watched all three of my children develop a strong sense of self. I am joyful for that vision. Whatever I have done or haven't done, you live with the freedom to create who you are.

Paul and I celebrated our 16th wedding anniversary. We watched the video, as we do every year. My cherubic seven-year-old, missing her two front teeth, clinging to me with adoration. Oh, how we twirled and danced that day. It would seem a beautiful life was ahead of us. How could I have known that, all these years later, there would come such a dire separation. If I had any inkling, I would have clung to you with more determination.

I won't defend the decades that I spoke love. Felt love. Screamed it, wrote it, e-mailed it, cried it, whispered it, and quietly thought it with great urgency. In return, an eerie silence. No argument, no challenge…

So, I waited. More mindful determination. The quiet hush of absence wafts over me like a thundercloud. More judgement, and a sense of foreboding. More people telling me what I've done wrong. A weird implication that my middle child is who she is, not as part of me, but in spite of me. And my wounds grow deeper.

The time that has passed leaves me with a weird sense that we are strangers. I know you by what others tell me. I view the internet, blogs, and study photos. Tears well in my eyes as I touch the screen, praying for you to reach back. How do I hold you? How do I stay in your life when I never left?

Gifts and monetary displays have become hollow. I am given the impression that I am pouring out and running dry. It never seems to matter what I do. Silence leaves me to assumption. And all the while I sit here with presents waiting for your footsteps to approach the front door. I strain my ears for the sound of your voice. I sit by the phone praying for it to ring. Four and a half years later, the baskets. balloons, trinkets, and checks wait for you to appear. My support remains steadfast, even though you refuse. So how do I reconcile the magnitude of opinions, while I quietly love you? My mother's heart continues to beat whether you are here or not.

A joyful time in all of our lives was Halloween. I chose a neutral theme to promote a sense of absurdity and silliness. If we can laugh together, perhaps we can also cry and dry each other's tears.

Dress up, adorn your classroom, eat candy and yell "Trick or Treat!!" Think of me when you wear the glasses with the big nose (above photo). And please remember:

You will never be too old to be cradled in the arms of your mother. This is where your life began. In an embrace that regards you with love, no matter what.

Love,
Mom

The following June I would fly to her so many continents and oceans away. At the time, I was unaware of the horrible reality. When estrangement becomes a solution, it is the first place we go at any sign of discomfort. Today, the deafening silence has accumulated, and we are estranged for the third time. Though this letter was written years ago, it fits our circumstances today. A startling truth to the repetitive power of unresolved conflict.

I remain cautious when I need to pour out emotions. I choose my audience. I have collected a posse who don't require me to have a line of defense. I have learned that the ability to express feelings is not a weakness. It's a strength without fear. It takes courage to own them.

The repetitive power of estrangement. My voice remains unheard.

They Want Crazy...Don't Give Them Crazy

(Christine Parsons Family Album)

THE MINUTE UNCOMFORTABLE emotions rise, everyone runs to separate corners. I think back to how I missed all of my youngest daughter's college years. But then a weird twist found great effort to communicate as graduation day approached. It seemed out of nowhere that my presence was needed in earnest. And like a mirage in the distance, I ran toward the source of water.

The years leading up to this moment began four years prior. A giant elephant moved into our living room and grew every time the father called for validation that he was A Parent. Abandonment was the basis of all our decisions, which created a path of least resistance. A survival tactic in order to avoid an elephant stampede.

This created a debilitating conflict that became greater than my ability for solutions. My daughter and I were at war, and there was no end for either one of us to claim a victory. My heart broke every time I was told I never cared or supported her in anything she did. All gratitude went to the father. And in comparison, I was a total failure. Exhausted and defeated, I reached out to the father. With my tail between my legs, I asked if our daughter could live with him and his wife for the summer following her freshman year.

My phone call was as if to say, "Congratulations, it's a girl." My relationship with him represented thirteen years of marriage, two daughters, and subsequent decades of mental exhaustion. I was constantly required to brain storm against his plays of counter parenting. It was psychological warfare with every interaction. I had to stay one step ahead. It was like living a game of chess with the unrelenting anticipation of his next move. Though his visits were sporadic, he washed doubt over every decision I made as the primary parent. I realize now that he was already planting seeds of my inability to be of sound mind.

We had both remarried, and his wife adopted the father's suggestion that I was completely inept. Though she never had a child, she knew exactly how a good and proper mother should act. Her judgment of me felt like burning flesh.

My husband and I were left to parent in the best way we knew how. All our effort went into minimizing the collateral damage. We never knew when the father would call. Sometimes weeks would pass without a word. This put us in a position to keep the mental unrest at bay, while making sure the inside of our home was a soft place to fall.

So here I was, fighting my desperation as I picked up the phone. I needed to believe that it was OK to ask the other parent for assistance. I, humbly, asked the father and his wife for a meeting. When we sat face to face, I stuttered the words, "Can Tiegan live with you for the summer?" And there it was. That Cheshire cat grin from the implication of my perceived failure. With a tone of superiority he pronounced, "Wow, too bad you don't get along. I have a great relationship with her. She listens to everything I say."

I remained silent as I took in the condescension. I closed my eyes to quiet my mind. Pushing my faith to be believe in myself as a kind and loving mother. I looked at the two people who considered every other Saturday sleepovers as a great effort in parenting. Seeing themselves as heroes for taking the girls on expensive vacations. Today the tale is told that they raised my daughter during those three summer months.

This was one of the most painful choices I have

ever had to make. The admission that I could not muscle my way through this conflict. I had to acknowledge the differences that had overtaken me and my precious baby girl. It felt like Sophie's choice.

Home had become a war zone. There were few moments of stillness. Though our love came without condition, my daughter kept a constant challenge that we sucked as parents. Accusations that we didn't care about her or support her interests. This brought on the implication that our son trumped her existence. "You can't wait for me to leave so you can have your little family!" Hearing this constant challenge resulted in his ongoing stomachache, and needing to run to the bathroom. The fear, guilt and shame of being our son became so severe that he lost ten pounds. He was just an eleven-year-old boy. At that point I knew something was about to break. It was as if a line was drawn in the sand. I had to save my boy. All the while knowing the call to the father would come with dire consequences. It was a horrible choice that needed to be made.

It shouldn't have been a surprise. The telling of the tale that rose from this experience was riddled with counter parenting. The accusation that I threw her out with no place to go. If the father hadn't stepped in to save her, she would have been out on the street. No mention of my plea for help. No indication that I asked for unity so we would finally work in the best interest of the child. No more tit for tat.

Instead of unity, all nineteen years of raising my daughter was obliterated. Someone actually said to me during that time, "So strange that Tiegan looks nothing like her mother." It was believed that the blonde blue-eyed stepmother was the one who gave birth. "So, who are the two children that you had with Derek?" The answer choked in my throat, as my motherhood felt denied.

From that point on, I was not invited into my daughter's life. Though I fought to hold on, it would be said that I only wanted to fight. The seeds of my mental instability were blossoming at a fast rate. Every attempt to engage was followed by an implication that my intention was to create further harm. This is when I truly began to understand the process of being set up to fail.

After all this, there was sudden ongoing communication. My daughter was a college senior, and she called to invite me to her graduation. Of course, my heart leaped with hope. But the reality of those silent years found me crying in despair. I had a horrible sense of foreboding. What horrors would find me, knowing I was not seen as the mother who raised her?

I grew more and more anxious as the date of the graduation moved closer on the calendar. That set up to fail feeling was ever present. I lived in a reality that I was perceived as a person with so many character defects, there were too many to count. If I tried to show up as Mom, I was reminded that my best was never enough.

At the reception following her graduation ceremony, everyone interacted with a familiarity—a comfort not mine, since I was a stranger to all of it. I watched "The Parents" preen themselves over the compliments expressed that day, "You have raised an amazing daughter." I was overcome by the knot in my stomach while listening to the parents of convenience accept accolades of their dedication.

There was no acknowledgment of my loving hands. Nothing mentioned about my physical presence, or how I showed up every day, even on the days when I didn't want to. No mention of my husband, a stepfather, who entered our circumstances filling the void of an undeniable absence. He graciously evolved into his new instant family, persevering with dignity through all the years of nightmarish blips, those horrible scenarios when the father decided to show up. Now we were living the reality of how all that mental unrest was a disaster in the making.

I tried in earnest to fit in. To work the crowd as if I belonged. But it was to no avail. The anticipated question was asked one too many times: "So how do you know Tiegan?" It became the straw that broke the camel's back. My anger rose like boiling water, and every bit of despair exploded, "Oh I am just the biological mother who decided to show up after twenty-two years!" And I left the party because I could not stop crying. That feeling of being invisible. Tapping the mic as though no one could hear me, "Is this thing on?"

I walked block after block trying to gain control of my anguish. Eventually, I had to admit the despair had taken over. My attempts to override it were fruitless. In anticipation of this doom, my husband and I had created a code word that would indicate the need for an immediate departure. DH, the abbreviation for dick head.

We broke the circle that surrounded the father and his wife. All so celebratory, everyone laughing a bit too hard. I could barely speak the words, "We have to go." They all looked at me like the crazy person they had created in my image. I remember turning on my heel and sprinting toward the car. My eldest daughter ran after me, grabbing my arm, "Don't do this." and through my wracking sobs I mustered, "I have to." It wasn't long before the story was told that I had ruined the entire graduation. Today I am humbled that I am given that much power.

Since then (that was 2007), I am able to recognize attempts to push me toward insanity. The culmination of these experiences has given me the ability to be calm in the middle of a storm. Looking back, I can see the emotional triggers being hurled at me. Shots fired, and notes taken in regard to my "inexplicable" acts of desperation. Claims that my crazy just comes from out of nowhere. Reasons to be cautious around me because no one ever knows when I am going to snap. "What the hell is wrong with her? She ruins every family gathering."

I gave them crazy that day. I admit it. More proof of being unworthy. It's still talked about. An example made of every incident that I was poked during times of weakness. They put my reactions under a microscope without any acknowledgement of the cause. My years of child rearing are not remembered with any warmth or devotion. My efforts have been twisted in recollection. The story is told as a tale of surviving my house filled with rage. They would have been safer with the other parent.

When we truly comprehend that we don't need to show up for every fight, we are empowered by our choices. Even if we are triggered, there is no need to respond. Silence can be used as a weapon, and it can also be used as a tool in the throes of conflict. Say nothing. Hit the pause button. Allow emotions to simmer. Go for a walk (bi-lateral "left-right" stimulation that engages both sides of the brain). Emotion + Logic = Mindful.

When they want crazy, don't give them crazy. I leave you with a favorite mantra: Never defend yourself. Your friends don't need it, and your enemies will believe it anyway.

Movement

(Christine Parsons Photo)

WHEN WE LEARN to cope with the silence, we learn to build a life that depends on it. We still pray for movement, a wiggle, or some sort of change. Our ears perk at the sound of a whisper. But the slightest audible tone has the ability to wretch our nervous system into overdrive.

I find I am most at peace without any information. It's easier to live my days knowing exactly what to expect. I have gained a sense of comfort through my daily human interactions. Staying connected with those who see me for who I am.

The problem with information, is when it's about my estranged adult children. This kind of news always comes unsolicited. There is no way to prepare. It makes my brain feel like an active beehive with a roaring buzz that I can't turn off.

Movement...it can be as simple as a photograph. Seeing a notification that you have received a message. Recognizing the name of the sender, and opening without hesitation or cause for concern. Your eyes adjust to look at the few photographs that pop out with the caption, "Thought you would want to see." And the assault to your senses ensues.

I was sent images of a two-year-old girl, and a five-year-old boy. At first, I was wondering who they were. An epic disaster. The photos were of my granddaughter's second birthday party. And the boy...my grandson. My offspring. Total strangers. No recognition, and now seeing them has created a greater divide. Just a few minutes prior, my heart had been safe. Every day I think of my cherubs as being far away. They live in an alternate universe where I hope to visit someday.

These images of my grandchildren also revealed my daughter's very pregnant belly. This is how I found out I was going to be the grandmother of five. Way too much movement. I want to go back to that moment of ignorance. To stand perfectly still without a whisper.

There are many innocent souls who feel the devastation of estrangement. I have shared my belief that it doesn't just hurt me. Though I am the person intended, there is an unwitting community who feels the pain. A horrible ripple effect.

I tell myself, as I have offered to other estranged parents, "Move away from anger." I admit that I fall prey. With full disclosure, I do have my moments. Days when I feel this is all too much to bear.

The question persists, "How can my daughters just turn me away?" But if I answer with bitterness, it only adds to a fire that is already burning. It is work to keep my thoughts away from resentment. I have to remind myself that I hate the behavior, not the people.

Movement. Though it may seem like cause for celebration, I find myself in pause. Fearful of getting sucked back into the past. Drastically reminded that I am not part of the present. Waking each day with hope of tomorrow.

There are definitely chapters in our history that require revisiting. This is with the intention to mend what is broken. Otherwise, the past remains present and determines the future. All of us are required to be accountable for what went wrong. We arrived here collectively, so to blame one person is counterproductive. We can only be better together, if we are together. We can unite through the purpose of creating change that moves us forward. Movement. It has all the potential of a beat I can dance to when it doesn't put me to bed.

It is the tough subjects that reveal the location of where the truth is buried. When we are able to work through the discomfort, we can find solutions. That process can provide new ways to resolve conflict without going back into silence. Putting the past where it belongs. Looking in the rear-view mirror only to see how far we have come.

Birth Days....

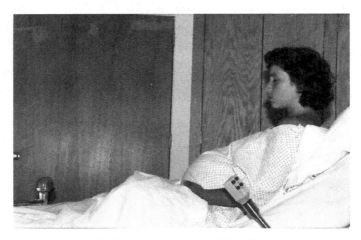

(Christine Parsons Family Album)

THERE IS NO denying that there are days on the calendar that provoke emotions deeper than others. I don't need to look at the display of months to know when these dates are approaching. Spring represents birthday season, and every year it spikes my nervous system.

I have been absent from my daughter's lives since 2016. In effort to gain equilibrium, I write letters that I sometimes send. And other times I keep my writing to myself to safely express my feelings. So much of what I know about my family comes as third-party news. Someone recently told me that Alice (the stepmother) is believed to be the biological grandmother. Simply put, "You've been replaced."

I am left to wonder how much of this is true, if true at all? But hearing it throws me into mourning. So much gets lost in the silence. The past few days have been a fight to rise above the assumptions. My efforts are with perseverance to get back to my truth. "I am a good, kind and loving mother, grandmother, wife, and friend." The following letter was written when I believed there was something I could say to change our circumstances. It remains true every day that I listen to this deafening silence.

>Dear Zoey,
>
>I have spent the past few days thinking about our recent text exchange. This journey of estrangement has left us subject to hearsay and conjecture. We receive these tidbits of information about each other, which forces us to guess what is true. It aligns us with judgment, because we really have no idea what the other is thinking or feeling.
>
>The distance between us has, understandably, heightened our fear that any contact will cause further harm. The quandary is that silence denigrates all that was good. The question now begs, "Is there anything left to salvage?"
>
>I am certain that together, we can provide each other with strength, hope, and courage.

Apart, these circumstances will remain unresolved, and resentment will build in all the things that are left unsaid. It will keep us in the past because there is no present or promise of a future.

We both wonder if this is fixable, and the not knowing keeps our relationship in limbo. My experience with doubt is anxiety, sleeplessness, and fear. If we are to arrive at irreconcilable differences, we should both be free of uncertainty.

As I said before, "I have faith that broken ends can mend." I am willing to take this journey with you to absolve all doubt. I will go to a counselor or mediator of your choosing. My hope is that we will both learn why and how this happened. If the present circumstances are inevitable, I am asking for a peaceful conclusion.

Love,
Mom

(No response)

Gather Your Posse

(Christine Parsons Photo)

THERE WAS A time when I could not align with the struggles of other parents of estranged adult children. I realized that I had created an identity around it, and lost all the other parts of who I am. Reading the plight of others flattened me, and all hope was lost.

It took a year for my search of self-discovery to reveal all of the different compartments that reside in my heart. There was room for plenty. Though I am a mother of estranged adult children, there is so much more. This is when I knew that the connection with other parents would lift me to higher ground. My showing of support gave me the courage to own every part of who I am.

I think of that scared, quivering mother that was once me. A lost soul crawling on my hands and knees begging for mercy. Screaming in a blinding hysteria, "Please let me see my grandchildren. Please give me back my family." Only to hear that my vulnerability was made to fit the mold of my insanity. Instead of screaming for my daughter, it was told I was screaming at my daughter. In that moment, I realized that every action and reaction would be twisted to have a different meaning. My therapist spoke to me softly, "In this situation, you can't do anything right."

I continue to grieve over that part of my story. I can tenderly recall the three years devoted to leaving no stone unturned. I was once of a notion that I could "fix" this. If only I could send the right text, buy the right gift…or say the right words. Certainly, there had to be an exact method that would unlock this fortress of pain.

The sad truth creeped in. I will never hold the key to anyone else's power to heal. Not even my own children. If we choose to hold tightly to a helium balloon, it will never be set free. It won't know the feeling of soaring on high. All the chemistry that gives this latex sphere the ability to take flight is denied. And so it goes with the pain of emotional conflict.

Keeping it close guarantees that it will stay right where it is. All energy is focused on a tight fist wrapped around the string that tethers the balloon. Releasing it comes with too much risk. The balloon has become a part of the daily routine. It represents comfort. The thought of watching it fly away is filled with fear of the unknown. Without realizing the significance, life revolves around that tight fist.

Each one of us has a story of profound moments that require recovery. If gone unreconciled, the nervous system will continue to react to those memories as if they happened yesterday. Past trauma needs a conversation...and yes, it is an emotional marathon to unearth these scenarios. But it is the only direct way to put the past to rest.... once and for all. Otherwise, it will keep showing up in the present and determine the future. Shaming someone else for the way we feel is not a solution. Wounds won't heal by singling out one person. Even if that someone was there at the onset of the trauma, they can't heal us from the experience.

All of our human interaction requires negotiation and compromise. If not, we find ourselves in a dictatorship with one person making all the rules. These rules are given definitively, though ever changing without warning. To distance with love does not mean love is denied. It is an action that demonstrates deep and powerful caring for one's self. It is to say, "I believe I am here with a purpose, and I write my own definition."

Surround yourself with beautiful things. Choose

the people who don't need to be convinced. They will greet you with sincerity free of judgment. Find those who are able to bestow the priceless gift of empathy. Gather your posse and circle the wagons.

The Ripple Effect

(Christine Parsons Photo)

THE THING ABOUT estrangement is that it doesn't just hurt the person intended. It hurts an entire community of those who care about you and your family.

We might be able to understand the issues that accumulated from raising children. Our history is a tale of surviving defeat and celebrating victories. No family is free of struggle. And through it all we believed that, no matter what, we would stick together, standing tall, and proud as the example of a united front.

When my first grandchild was born, my heart celebrated the emotions that washed over me. This innocent babe was like a glimmering star. A brilliant light that shined over every hard decision I had to make as a parent. I believed that each new offspring would heighten those feelings, and my beloved home would be rich from the experience.

And then it all went silent. Somehow all those issues left unspoken became a mountain too high to climb. The sound of my screams could be heard from every corner. It was death right before my eyes. It was like watching my family get hit by a train. Everywhere I looked, there was carnage from the accident of estrangement.

I call it an accident because there was no planning. What could have prepared me? I am a loving mother who made decisions based on the best interest of her children. How could I just be gone, dismissed and disregarded? In minutes, estrangement had spread into every aspect of my life.

I can't begin to calculate the loss. There is no prevention in stopping the spread. Every encounter happens in the shadows of my reality. After visiting with a friend, she walked me to my car. In parting she said, "I just want you to know that your daughters are the elephant in the living room. Every time I see you, I want to ask, but then I don't. Please know that every person who cares about you feels the sadness." The ripple effect. It's like trying to hold water in your hands. Eventually, it seeps through your fingers, trickling on to the floor, and everything in its path gets wet.

Freya

(Christine Parsons Family Album)

MY RELATIONSHIP WITH my mother was so many things. The warmth of her nurturing found me grabbing on with both hands as I immersed myself in her love. I focused on these moments when she was beauty and light.

The darkness of her demons taught me a lot about unresolved conflict. When we harbor bitterness and resentment, it truly does become the bitter pill we swallow, hoping an ill fate for someone else.

My mother's fight against her demons would be her demise. The attack against people who were no longer there created a life filled with resentment. She was rarely at peace. Unresolved conflict became a cancer. The unrelenting bitterness robbed her body, mind and spirit of any joy. Her death, at age fifty-seven, was a slamming door. Our battles were left for me to resolve on my own. It was a huge task to free myself of generations past. Throwing away the baggage of their inability to meet conflict face to face. Estrangement was my role model. Now, it seems a giant rut that I was unable to avoid.

I wrote this poem in memory of my mother. It acknowledges that our lives are given to us with a choice and an opportunity. For me, things haven't exactly turned out like I had hoped. But who doesn't wish for the ability to reconstruct a memory? It's as if we could manifest a time machine, and go back to the past. Once there, we could rewrite chapters that hold hurt and trauma. I push myself to remain present, as all of my experiences become part of who I am. My choice, as I face adversity, is to shine on.

SHINE ON
The silence cried
and I fell to earth.
My mother whispered
"You are of worth."

As defined by others
her desperate plea,
"Be who you are,
the best of me."

My journey of self,
is a constant quest.
My anger and doubt
shall be put to rest.

My world is authentic,
loving and kind.
Chaos is created
in bitter minds.

Before you speak
know it's true.
To judge is a decision
with limited view.

NEVERTHELESS THEY PERSISTED

Cast off the mean
and draw in the good.
Minus you, the world
would be not as it should.

Be kind, be assertive,
stay focused on right.
Shine on, sparkle free,
you are the light.

Mother's Day

(Jeffrey Simpson Photo)

THERE WAS A time when my heart was so broken, I would bristle when asked, "Do you have children?" My answer was a lie: "Yes, I have a son," despite the truth. I, also, have two daughters. The denial of their existence always sat wrong in my nervous system... and I would walk away feeling sick. But my reality appeared as a double-edged sword. Speaking out loud and revealing that I have no relationship with my adult daughters was equally disturbing. It provoked that look of, "What horrible thing did you do?" And when that happened, I would stutter in defense, which sounded crazy...making me feel even worse.

There came moments of grave doubt. "How do I

keep living a life filled with such despair?" It was my belief that I had to accept a life of anguish and a deepening fall into darkness. I became a mere shadow of the person I once was. I felt that I had to give away my power to give permission for others to write my definition. The estrangement came with a demand that I needed to change...but change into what? The truth is that I will never be the same.

Nothing productive has yet to be spoken. Despite my pleading, "I love you. I want you in my life. What do I have to do to move us to a better place? What is the change you wish to see?" I began to realize my perceived character defects were not an answer nor a solution. All sentences began with "you"...and never "we." Our human relationships depend on two or more people interacting. Disagreements don't happen with one person. Estrangement is collective, and we all participated in what went wrong. Everyone needs to show up to work the problem. How can we be better together, unless we are together? Healing fragmentation can't happen if we all remain in separate corners.

Since 2016, my daughters have decided that their lives and the lives of their children are better off without me. This was never my choice, and now I understand it is not mine to fix. I no longer defend myself. Especially for the person I was five minutes ago, never mind last week or even decades earlier. I would not shame my daughters for the temper tantrums they had when they were three. They are no longer those people, and neither am I.

When I hear the expression: "You should have known better." The truth is as plain as day. We cannot gain the knowledge we will need for tomorrow until it is yesterday. We make decisions based on our ability for greater intelligence. Each one of us is in constant transition to the people we are yet to become. It is counterproductive to hold someone's feet to the fire for something that is already written. There are no do-overs. Productive dialogue is spoken with the intention to move us forward. We need only use the past as a reference to develop better skills. Old hurt and trauma don't need to keep showing up in the present to determine our future. The power of resolving conflict identifies the issues...and heals the emotions once and for all. And this is when hope springs eternal.

As an estranged mother of adult children, I continue to pray for light to shine in dark places. I am here, as I have always been. My lap is never too small for my children to rest. My arms are never too short to envelope with love. My ears never too deaf to hear the promise of "us." I stand proud as the mother of three. This is a huge part of who I am and not to be denied.

I wish all of my readers days filled with joy. May you celebrate every bit of who you are. My hope is that you commit to this all day, every day. Our lives as parents do not require a random Sunday to validate this journey and our choices. I know you are always doing your best, and tomorrow you will do even better.

How to Fix Estrangement

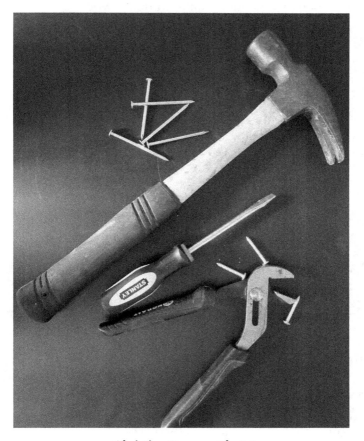

(Christine Parsons Photo)

SO OFTEN, WE grab hold of any book, article, podcast, or reference to how we might "fix" estrangement. We have all tried to apologize, send loving texts, cards, gifts...anything that represents our parenthood and good intentions. We are willing to own failure, perceived abuse, abandonment...whether it's true or not. Though we might have been told that our best was never good enough, what does that really mean?

The accusations of the pain we caused ten years ago...twenty years ago...or maybe even last week creates feelings of being powerless. So many sentences beginning with shoulda, woulda, coulda. All in effort to reconstruct memories that keep us gripped in the past without any wiggle room to move us forward. Though we might have been there when the emotional conflict began, we can't stop our children from holding on. They have the control over the release button.

As estranged parents, we are so eager to gather information that will move us toward reconciliation. But this requires our estranged child to show up. They have to be ready to do the emotional work. Everyone involved must speak a productive dialogue that is meant to heal.

True and trustworthy reconciliation requires everyone to give 100% of who they are. And here is when we pray for our adult children to shine light in dark places. We will "fix it" when everyone is ready to gain emotional intelligence. There is no pretending that estrangement hasn't happened. It feels a bit terrifying, the thought of unearthing past wounds and revisiting our most painful chapters. It's like ripping off a Band-Aid. The skin reacts, but eventually we see the healing that was happening beneath.

When estrangement was first threatened, my best defense was to remain calm. I would hit "pause" so my words would be concise and rational. I was being shamed for yesterday before it all went silent. This solution has proved to create more conflict.

The question begs, "What can I fix?" The answer is me. Self-care is what matters most. We are of no use to anyone, least of all ourselves, if we are broken. I leave you with this mantra:

Your mind will believe everything you tell it. Feed it faith. Feed it truth. Feed it love.

When It Becomes Necessary to Distance with Love

(Jeffrey Simpson Photo)

I HAVE READ articles that advise the estranged parent to never give up. To keep pouring out love. To keep sending texts, gifts, and e-mails. To stay connected on social media despite the pain of seeing lives gone on without you. But what happens when this effort becomes detrimental to self? The assault on the heart when there is no response. Or worse, all of your intentions of loving kindness are returned with more anger. I reached that place after three years. My efforts did not create change for the better. My suggested solutions only proved to heighten anger or just more silence. My therapist quietly offered, "Everything you do makes them mad." And this was the absolute truth. In order to save myself, I had to preserve the relationships that were right in front of me. This required me to distance with love. The following letter was sent after my realization. I can't heal my family by myself.

Dear Zoey and Tiegan,
What started out as days, became months, and now years. The time has evolved and I must come to terms with a harsh truth. If you wanted this to get better, we would have had long and difficult conversations. Instead, choices are being made, based on where you place the most value. I am learning to live with this. Without discussion, a verdict has been reached, and the case is closed. The conclusion is that I am an abusive parent. There was a brief moment, when I believed you. I found myself crawling on hands and knees, re-evaluating the person I am, and the seeds I have sown. Was I getting what I deserved? A journey of discovery led me back to the place

where I began. I am a good, kind, and loving mother. I am an incredible grandmother.

There has been much discussion about my anger, bitterness, and resentment. I guess the tendency is to mirror what we see. There is much of it, and it seems to come from all sides. Yes, there is a lot of crap that will remain part of who we are. But the events that have happened to us, as a family, can't hinge on one person. I won't shoulder this by myself. It is collective, and it is work. Talking about feelings is not a shortcoming. It is the vast difference between chaos and peace.

I am not weak, I am not overly emotional, and I am not mentally unstable. I am human, and beautifully flawed. I hear you when you tell me you have been hurt. I have been hurt, too. Tit for tat. Estrangement, however, is not problem-solving; it is problem-causing. It is historical and will keep getting passed down. I have become the living proof. I believed that I could change this horrible pattern, and so, I became a verbal processor. I admit, I have a pervasive need for conflict resolution. This is a quest that was born of my emotions from losing my whole family at the tender age of eight. My adults were incapable. They didn't know how to do anything else. It was what they were taught.

I have, reluctantly, accepted that it was never up to me to change the course of where my family would go. The propensity to take silence to the grave is a strong and powerful force. It is built within our genes. I had high hopes that I could move us forward. I tried with everything I had. I felt failure. It is now up to you. In the meantime, so much is lost, and it is a choice.

I will remain right here, where I have always been. I am ready to begin uncomfortable conversations whenever you are ready. I never wanted this, and I can't fix it. Whatever happens to us in the future will rest on every decision yet to be made.

Love,
Mom

(No response)

Reconciliation

(Jeffrey Simpson Photo)

WE IMAGINE THAT moment. Running through a field of wild-flowers. Falling into each other's arms. Like a movie, all is forgiven, and so easily we just move on, desperately wanting to go back to another place in time. But once estrangement becomes a solution, it also becomes part of our story. This chapter is written.

I find the word "reconciliation" to be simple, because it implies an easy process. A belief that we just need to pick up the phone, send a text, or meet for coffee. An unwritten rule to leave all the hurt behind though our emotions are laced with fear. Every breath is an effort to pretend that bad things never happened. Unwittingly, we have moved the elephant into our living room. Quietly, we tiptoe around it, walking on eggshells so we won't make it mad. One wrong word, that tone of voice, or that face you make...and the elephant stampedes in a rage so familiar.

The truth is, we have no power over our adult children, and we cannot make them want for better. Going silent actually takes effort. It is with a willingness to hold on to the things that cannot be changed. But what can be gained by targeting one person for a perceived failed relationship?

As estranged parents, it is crucial to spend this time with focus on your own mental, spiritual, and physical health. The stress of carrying this load can take its toll. I still experience grave moments of doubt and insecurity. I have days when the pain is so great, I can't even get dressed. Those of us who have grandchildren could never have prepared for the suffering loss of grieving for those precious babes who are still alive. But if we allow ourselves to be robbed of our own self-worth, we lose our grasp on the power of choice.

If you are traveling this path, there might come a realization. You may have experienced that nothing you do or say creates any change. It is a leap of faith to trust, believing that our adult child will reach out when they are ready to move forward. Showing up with the commitment to fight fairly. Speaking words that are meant to heal. Having the courage to push away from the past rather than pulling toward it.

When we learn a new and productive way to reconcile our differences, we build on a foundation of a true and trustworthy reconciliation. Otherwise, we will tiptoe, feed the elephant, and continue on a journey paved with eggshells.

In the meantime, if the inclination is to send a card...do it. If nothing seems appropriate...do it. Try to unburden your mind of expectation. Spend your efforts doing whatever it takes to calm your nervous system. Concentrate on your own wellbeing.

This is not your fault, and it is not yours to fix. Estrangement is collective and requires everyone involved to show up and work the problem. Make self-care your mission. Give it purpose without regret.

Set Up to Fail

(Ariella Neville Photo)

I WAS GOING to be a grandmother for the second time. The love I already felt for my grandson was over the moon and back. His chubby little hands would cup my face: "GG, are you so happy?" "Oh, yes, baby." I would reply. But there were already waves of estrangement washing over these moments. My daughter was holding me at arm's length. Strange comments were made in regard to my behavior. I began to feel uneasy. The experience of my first adult child estrangement seemed all too familiar. My younger daughter and I acted like we were "together". But the truth was that nothing between us had been reconciled. Sadly, I realized I was continuing on a path paved with egg shells. This time with my eldest child.

As my daughter's belly grew, so did my sense of foreboding. I felt like I was on a train with no brakes. Nothing could stop this speeding force from crashing. Everything I believed to be true was about to run off the rails and implode. Though I would speak, my words floated into air. The father's wife was taking ownership of both of my daughters. I might have been OK with her attempt, but it seemed she was being given the power to override my motherhood. Everything she did was perfect, while I... well, too many character flaws to mention. It was as though I was constantly drunk. My equilibrium was off, and I just kept stumbling.

As my daughter's due date approached, I talked to a couple of her friends. Since this was her second child, I saw no need for a full-on baby shower. I shared my thoughts about celebrating my daughter and giving gifts meant just for her. I could not have prepared myself for what was about to happen.

I was checking my e-mail when the Evite accosted my senses. Home alone, I was shaking as I opened the contents. "Alice invites you to a baby shower for Zoey." I was being invited by the stepmother to my own daughter's celebration. I had no time to get over the shock, when another e-mail came directly from Alice, "....and why don't you go ahead and invite your husband?" Are you kidding me right now? Bring the man who raised our daughters? A suggestion that if she hadn't extended a welcome, he would have been excluded? The pain in my heart was so excruciating, I wanted to rip off my own skin.

This baby shower was becoming a gargantuan "set up to fail" scenario. I was well aware that no matter what I did, it would be ill fated. I was doomed...and I knew it. The devil and the angel were pulling me in two different directions. These invitations represented the demise of my family. The whispers in my ear were so conflicting: "Don't go." And to the contrary: "You have to go." and I couldn't wrap my brain around it. I wasn't asked to contribute, and there was no invitation to act as though I had any biological connection. So how? How to attend this occasion as any other guest?

The conflict I felt was that old familiar feeling of a nervous breakdown. Though I agreed to "show up," I wasn't sure in what state I would represent my motherhood. In a twist, perhaps created by my misgivings, we got ridiculously lost.

I didn't have a smartphone or GPS. It was a tourist area, and no one was able to direct us. So, we circled around the same area for half an hour. It was a blinding search for the street of this beach house where we had never been. I felt frantic, and feared an inability to not show up at all. And finally, we came upon someone who could give us clear instructions. As we turned onto the right street, my little flip phone rang.

It was my youngest daughter, not worried...but angry that we were late. The implication suggested that we were not lost, and our tardiness was with intention.

As I walked through the door, Alice exclaimed, "We are so happy you made it." I was shaking because my daughters stood behind her, waiting to for me to say something inappropriate. "Well, thank you for inviting me." I know. It was a bit snarky, and innocent just the same. My girls erupted in volume, "WOW, MOM, REALLY?!!"

Disgraced, I looked around the tiny room of fifteen women sitting elbow to elbow. It was a beautiful summer day, and there was a huge yard outside. Why was this gathering in such a confined space? I felt instant nausea. The circle of women seemed an impenetrable force. My eyes darted around the room to find a seat. There was no way to be graceful in that moment. Though I had taken two Xanax, it wasn't enough. I couldn't breathe, and therefore couldn't speak.

The only available seat was beside Alice's mother. I was already aware that this woman despised me. Though she had never bothered to know me, her judgment was palpable. She treated me as a bumbling fool, so inept she actually felt sorry for my daughters. And so, she spouted with disdain from the corner of her mouth, "Hello, Christine." Much like Jerry Seinfeld when meeting face to face with Newman, and I held back tears.

Once seated with my husband beside me, Alice

prompted him to join "The Men" down at the beach. He knew I was in distress, but it was a no-win situation. These scenarios were so common. I was already ruining the party. He squeezed my hand, and I felt helpless as he walked out the door. The follow up phone call that came days later would unearth all my vulnerability: "Your face was so ridiculous. It was all like, please don't leave me. These people might kill me."

The shower proceeded like a bad horror movie. I watched the display of this barren stepmother playing Mommy. It came as a huge sense of relief when my pregnant daughter asked if I could take my then two-year-old grandson to the outdoor shower. My husband had brought him back from the beach. Too much sand was caked in "his business" and he needed to change clothes.

I can't really explain the intention of those who remained inside. I guess from the way I was being treated, everyone saw me as an afterthought. While we were out showering my grandson, drying him off, and putting on his clean clothes, Alice served the cake. We walked into the house to find the party breaking up. Some were leaving and others just headed outside. I looked at the empty plate filled with a few crumbs and frosting. My senses were overcome with feelings of being nonexistent. So, my behavior followed, and I acted accordingly. I tried so hard to not give them crazy, but my despair took over.

As I was barely able to hold back tears, my husband took the cue and we left. Within a week, the shaming phone calls began. The conclusion, "I don't know how you walk around being the way you are. So mentally unstable. If you can't honor my father and Alice, we will estrange from you!!"

When my granddaughter was born, it came in the wake of this chaos. By then, it was impossible for me to respond correctly to the announcement of her birth. I didn't visit soon enough. I didn't act right when I got there. My behavior so unacceptable I was told to leave my daughter's home. Another walk of shame, as I headed to the door. Alice and her mother sat there gleefully doing everything right.

I tried to pretend that my grandchildren ensured my presence. But as a child born into estrangement, I knew I was kidding myself. At the age of eight, as an only child, I had grandparents, uncles, aunts, and cousins. We gathered for Sunday dinners, and the comfort of extended family was my soft place to fall. But then it all went silent. The adults got mad. They were incapable of considering the impact on the children. I didn't see them again until I was seventeen. By then, I had listened to years of my parent's rages, and no longer trusted any of my relatives to have my best interest at heart.

I hung on to my daughters by a thread for the next two years. Inevitably, as hard as I tried, estrangement was the solution. I was the tumor that needed to be eradicated in order to preserve the rest of the family.

As you might expect, I haven't done estrangement right. I shouldn't have told anyone. Any "normal" person would have just gone off quietly into the night holding onto their shame. The decision was made. I am a failure at motherhood, and tanked miserably with my every intention.

But if someone says, "You're a failure," is it true? I have learned never to give anyone permission to define who I am. Each one of us is a loving parent who made decisions based on their best knowledge. There is no way to jump ahead with the information you will need for tomorrow...until it is yesterday. This makes it possible to face adversity from a place of strength.

I have spent these past years working at finding my place of compassion. The release of anger, bitterness and resentment frees me of the debilitating shame and guilt. I was told that I needed to change. The truth is, we are all in constant transition of the people we are yet to become. Forgive yourself for yesterday.

Grieving

(Jeffrey Simpson Photo)

WHEN YOU GRIEVE for people who are still alive, their geographical location is no matter. Pictures reveal lives gone on without us. We know that our estranged children are having relationships with other people. It provokes emotions of feeling nonexistent when social media reveals gatherings. I have since blocked both of my daughters and their extended family. Pop-ups in my news feed required days for me to recover.

I was told that my younger daughter moved out west. It was an offering of information about my own child. Hearing the words spilling from the lips of an acquaintance because of a belief that by knowing, I would somehow feel better. Perhaps closer. And yet, these are all the things I wish to un-hear. I'd rather not know. My ignorance keeps me safe. Third-party news from the well-intended is like nails on a chalk board. I want to scream, "Please stop talking!" I have no idea how to process constructively. Do I own it? Do I take these fragments and create a story? Pretend that I know where and how my adult children tend to their other relationships? Do I have bragging rights?

My eldest daughter lives two hours away. I could easily do a drive-by. But I tried that once, and showed up unannounced. Hoping that by seeing me, she would be jarred back to a time before estrangement. That was not to be. My grandson, four at the time, was the only one who responded with a cheerful welcome. My granddaughter, two at the time, had no idea who I was. And feeling the tension, she buried her face in her mother's chest.

"GG, come see our Christmas tree," the wee boy chattered before his dad had to drive him to school. "Will you be here when I get home?" he asked me, doe-eyed. I told him probably not, but I hoped to see him again soon.

Though that drive-by initiated brief contact, the unresolved conflict was still there. Two days before I was due to come and watch my grandson's ski lesson, my daughter sent an e-mail asking me to stay away. That was January of 2017.

Geography. The location. Knowing where they live, or not knowing? Which pain is less?

While imagining reconciliation, I am keenly aware of the commitment it will take to meet face to face and speak the issues. There is no way we can pretend that bad things never happened. The effort of sweeping our pain under the rug, creates a large bulge that we will trip over at the first sign of trouble. Unresolved conflict, whether we want it to or not, demands attention.

Without a productive dialogue, the tendency to keep beating up the past will be ongoing. There are chapters in our history that need to be revisited in order to heal. Otherwise, future chapters will be written with greater conflict. I refer to these circumstances as the Estrangement Elephant.

A giant gray mammal is sitting in the middle of the living room. Ignoring him proves to antagonize. He grows larger, angrier, and more comfortable. The presence becomes an immovable force. Our instinct is to tip toe around it. Confrontation seems terrifying. We don't want him to fly into a rage, destroying everything in his path. But if we can override fear, replace it with love, we can greet conflict like a good friend. Working the problem together opens the opportunity to evolve with kindness, empathy, and compassion.

GRIEVING

United as a family, we can push the elephant out of the house once and for all.

Grieving. Wishing to tell a different story. Or perhaps moving the focus to the horizon. Praying for the opportunity to write chapters of healing. And so, we continue to pray for light to shine in dark places. Keep the faith. Remove doubt. The whole world awaits you...

Christmas

(Christine Parsons Family Album)

GIFTS FOR THE grandchildren? A token for the estranged adult child? What should I do? Keep pouring out pieces of my soul? Plagued by the question, "If I don't reach out, will it be another reason to banish me in silence?"

My therapist said to me a few years ago, "What's the worst that can happen? They will stop speaking to you? They won't let you see your grandchildren?" I realized I was already living the worst.

My life had to evolve based on that truth. As an estranged parent, birthdays, holidays, and special events become cause for fear and anxiety. When the people we love choose to see the worst of who we are, they blind themselves to all the good. We are stuck in this notion to do what's right. Do something that will create change. And the effort feels like pushing rope uphill. The mindset eventually changes. Do what feels right inside your own body. Do whatever calms your nervous system.

This journey is not up for judgment or criticism. There can be no rules. There is no right or wrong. Honor your heart. Soothe your soul. Buy gifts if that feels right. Send texts, money, or cards. And the minute it leaves your hands, set if free. Remove expectations so you won't be disappointed or hurt.

I have had to come to a full comprehension that my family is not ready to heal. I trust that they will reach out the moment they choose to do the emotional work. In the meantime, I work on remaining calm. I am best when I feel peaceful. Every once in a while, I send a text or an e-mail. The minute I press send, I set the intention free.

I pray that you find peace through the holidays. The coming weeks are filled with an ideal that represents a giving spirit. I believe these circumstances require us to give ourselves what others don't have. Nourish your soul with joy. Buy a silly sweater. Be with people who greet you with sincerity. Surround yourself with beautiful things. Celebrate what life is while you walk tenderly around what you thought it would be. Tiny miracles will manifest when you open your arms to all that is possible.

Historical Hysteria

(Christine Parsons Family Album)

I AM THE product of estrangement. It is, therefore, my belief that the behavior of our adult children is nothing new. It is not bound to a 21st century mindset of entitlement. It is not born out of being spoiled or too nurtured. It isn't really about abuse either. Estrangement is the result of unresolved conflict. A human factor that has existed since the dawn of time. It is an inability to pinpoint the events that caused the emotions.

Screaming pain will never evolve into healing. Blaming another person for the way we feel can't become anything else other than blame. Firing out guilt and failure won't move us forward. Sadly, to the contrary, our feet will remain firmly planted in the past. It will stay present and determine the future.

As a survivor of abuse and subsequent recovery from addiction, I can honestly share that I once lived the mindset of blame. I believed my every hardship was my parents' fault. Their best wasn't good enough, and I deserved better. So, my own self-destruction and unhealthy choices were my revenge on them. I was motivated to bring myself to the precipice of death. And once standing on that edge, I was terrified to die. My bottom. My epiphany. My light bulb.

Yes, my parents are dead, but I still wish they'd change. This notion speaks to the preposterous. Is there any possibility that they will rise and re-write my history? Can they give me those fairy tale memories instead of my tormented reality? I needed to feel safe, loved, and secure. But that childhood is not my story. What I am left with is the truth. There is no amount of shame, blame, guilt, or even self-destruction that will heal my own heart. No one can solve me, nor can I solve anyone else. Not even my own children.

When I think of my daughters, I am able to find compassion. My past has evolved me away from anger. Their pain is not my fault. Unresolved conflict needs a lot of uncomfortable conversations. It needs to speak the issues...not the feelings. This requires tools and the skills to use them. Once acquired, we can build a new house. Otherwise, we will remain on a foundation created of instability.

Adult Child Estrangement is not about hatred. It is more about past trauma that pushes us to hand our unpleasant emotions over to someone else. My hindsight allows me to "see" all the misguided communication over decades. The right fighting, hitting below the belt, kill or be killed, and believing that the one who screamed the loudest won. But just because it's loud, doesn't make it true.

As a student of human behavior, my lessons have blossomed through my experience. It is very difficult to watch our loved ones carry an unnecessary burden. A nagging question persists: "How long and how far do you want to carry this?" I pray for the moment my daughters will respond, "Not one more day, and not one more step."

The above photo was taken in 1960. It shows me holding the ball surrounded by family. These gatherings with extended family offered me great comfort. I had no way to prepare for the day when it seemed they just disappeared. I was in my late teens when they all reunited, but they continued to walk on eggshells. The past estrangement just led to the next one, and the right words were never spoken. It was their answer to unresolved conflict. They took their silence to the grave. It was a history I had hoped not to repeat.

Weathering the Tide

(Christine Parsons Photo)

WHEN PEOPLE USED to say, "Your daughters will come around," my response was, "What if they don't?" In other words, I had to learn how to reap the glory of opportunity given to me each day. I was missing all of life's blessings by looking toward tomorrow without ceasing the moments of now. My husband took me by the shoulders and said, "You still have me...our son, and so many dear friends who care about you."

I was of no use to anyone if I was broken, least of all myself. My estranged daughters are practicing free will. It has a mind of its own. This is not a scraped knee or a bruised elbow. My love cannot heal the pain that lives within my children's hearts. The second any of us adopts this as our own, is the moment we circle the drain. Suddenly sucked into a vortex that everything is our fault, which is impossible. Relationships are not individual...they are collaborative. They are healthy when there is a willingness to compromise and negotiate.

The decision to take it all on our shoulders is like building a house on sand. It is to sit on the shore, holding our breath, watching the tide, and hoping to ward off a mighty wave. Inevitably, the house washes away as the ebb and flow ravages the foundation of everything unstable. We can free our own heart when we release ourselves from the burden of blame. This is not your fault.

I have a friend who lost her son in death. She said to me, "As long as they are alive, there is hope." And I hold this close to my chest. In the meantime, I allow the silence of knowing that my love is not what's in question. It is self-love that empowers us to work our own problems. We understand the boundaries we cross when we attempt to solve other people. It's not our business nor our work to reconcile someone else's resentments. The choice to remain in anger is a choice. And blame will never become anything else.

We pray for the light of self-love to shine in our children. We wait for the miraculous warmth that will envelope us in truth. The process of forgiving ourselves lends us an ability to be brave no matter what the change in tide.

My Feelings About Regret

(Jeffrey Simpson Photo)

EMOTIONAL PARALYSIS. WE wouldn't ask a person in a wheel chair to get up and walk. It is the same thing when we expect someone who can't emote to talk productively about feelings. This is waiting for the cat to bark. People can't give us what they don't have.

MY FEELINGS ABOUT REGRET

We are faced with our children's perception that doesn't align with our reality. There is no line of defense. Just non argumentative responses like: "I am so sorry that you feel this way. We, apparently, have a difference of opinion."

To travel down a road of regret, will only be met with self-deprecation and relinquishing every bit of who we are. Each one of us carries unsavory moments. Our circumstances indicate that we were not doing our best, when it is experience that teaches us to do better. There are no failures. They just become lessons that evolve with the information. Once learned, we are able to proceed with greater intelligence.

Whenever I feel myself slipping toward that daunting feeling of being powerless, an inner voice speaks clearly: "Don't hand yourself over. Don't give away the keys to your house. Forgive yourself for yesterday."

Each one of us is in constant transition of the people we are yet to become. A life lived without regret is a life filled with purpose. This is not your fault. Estrangement is not your choice, and therefore not yours to fix. If you give your pain a purpose, you will gain a sense of direction, and the ability to proceed in kindness. The only other alternative is to use pain to create more. Be the light. Accept what is. Be brave.

Holding On

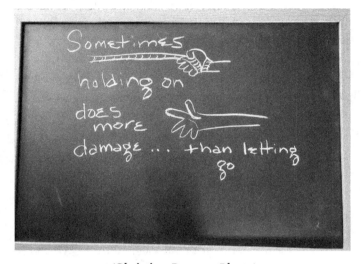

(Christine Parsons Photo)

"THANK YOU FOR never giving up on me," says the estranged child to the broken-hearted, exhausted parent. I have read advice that tells the desperate mother or father to keep vigilant by sending messages of devotion. I have read stories of parents breaking through the barrier of silence. Due, in part, to a daily commitment of pouring out pieces of who they are, no matter what the cost. The implication surmises that all things are suddenly forgiven. Did their emotional conflict just disappear? We already know the story of how they fell down. I want to know how they got back up. If the adult child is still assigning blame, they will show up as the same person that left.

I do admit, I was once relentless in my pursuit of opening a dialogue. I held on with both hands, searching for that highly coveted place of reconciliation. I spoke all the words that reiterated my unconditional love. And for me, at long last, I had to come to terms with the truth. My efforts came at the cost of my own detriment. Nothing I said brought any change. Our circumstances remained the same. There was a precise moment when I had to ask myself, "When is enough, enough?"

"Thank you for never giving up on me." These are the words I wish I could speak to my children. I wish I could have a concrete recollection of them pouring out pieces of who they are in effort to keep our family whole. If only I could erase the foregone conclusion that there is nothing about me worthy of redemption. But the months have turned into years. And still a deafening silence.

I see clearly the people who never gave up on me, because they never left. They held my hand when I needed it most. They sat with me in my sadness. In their company, I have never felt the need to defend myself or apologize for just being me.

My effort to change our circumstances was a self-deprecating pursuit. My offspring insisted that I am the villain in this story. I was deemed a leopard that could not change her spots. I was falling fast and hard down the rabbit hole. My therapist begged, "You have to find a way to stop. You just keep re-traumatizing yourself." I realized my hands had become bloody in my refusal to let go. I was slowly going insane. It was from that low place in my existence that I developed the ability to distance with love. I had to save myself and proudly identify exactly who I am: a good, kind and loving mother, grandmother, wife, and friend.

The years leading up to estrangement found me tiptoeing quietly around the truth of a painful past. My belief was: "If we don't talk about it, it will just go away." A wise woman offered me this nugget: "Everything that challenges you becomes your teacher." Unresolved conflict challenges my every instinct to verbally process. These lessons are my own. There is no way to force the process on someone else.

When our children are ready, we will finally speak the issues: "What are the reasons we fell into silence?" We will peel the onion layer by layer, healing past trauma by identifying the event that caused such deep emotion. It will happen when it becomes a decision.

Healthy relationships are built of negotiation and compromise. So, when you feel you should never give up, ask yourself, "Has my child given up on me?" If the answer is, "yes," it is time to save your own heart and distance with love.

Muddled in Confusion

(Ariella Neville Photo)

LIFE DOES NOT come without challenge. Blame is an instinct and keeps the truth at bay. It will buy you time. It will offer a temporary relief and alleviates personal accountability.

I have felt debilitating anger, believing that my hurt is someone else's fault. I stayed in pursuit of the person who caused me harm. It seemed a righteous quest. "People" need to feel my wrath and be held accountable for all the wrongs I have suffered. Revenge was ever present in my thought process. But this eventually found me in a downward spiral of my own making. The blame was hurting me more than the experience that created the emotional conflict. This instinct of "kill or be killed" was killing me.

In that spiral of self-destruction, I wasn't ready to accept that my process was ill fated. I continued to hand over my emotional pain to others. I carried a vengeance in my heart for all the horrible people who had mistreated me. They would know my fury!! And so, I swallowed the poisonous pill of resentment and waited for them to fall. And I waited...and I waited...and I waited....

My blame should have set them on fire. Or so I thought. And, finally, I began to realize my fragility of power. Giving someone the stink eye might offer some relief, but it is fleeting and temporary. The truth will check in on reality. Though we may try to blame others, our emotional pain is a choice.

As estranged parents, we have been on the receiving end of blame. We have been placed on a seat of accusations of inadequacy. The instinct is to mirror it back. Estrangement hurts. So many contributing factors. There is a desperate need to find fault when our emotions are in chaos.

We have experienced devastating thoughts of precious time wasted. Praying for productive dialogue. Waiting for that moment of discovery. And the sad truth creeps in. Blame never evolves. It might feel like it moves us forward, but the scenery stays the same.

It is our work to recognize how hurt people hurt

people. The path chosen by our adult children does not come with peace of mind. Holding on to unresolved conflict manifests in other places. It comes out in other relationships and behavior. There is no way to claim irreconcilable differences without an exhaustive effort to reconcile. It requires a commitment of no stone left unturned.

Our families need to put together a collective energy. Though there is a prevalent belief to leave the past behind, it will continue to mask the painful chapters that remain unresolved. All those emotions result in yelling to be heard. But just because it's loud doesn't make it true. Screaming ensures a hot pursuit of knee-jerk reactions. And we will just keep kicking each other.

Think of how this same statement will sound in a calm tone: "This is how I felt in that moment," instead of screaming, "You made me feel…." When we're mad, we act mad. When our mind is at peace, the behavior will follow. A family muddled in confusion can gain clarity by speaking the issues. Putting blame to rest will begin the path to healing.

Finding Solid Ground

(Christine Parsons Photo)

I FELT AS though the foundation of everything I had built was suddenly on sand. As much as my feet struggled to find solid ground, my footsteps for progress kept sinking. The effort of moving forward became impossible.

Though I begged for words that heal, in repetition, I was reminded of all things that made me void of redemption, clutching my ears because it was more than I could bear.

It was as if my heart had turned into molten lava. It continued to beat, but it burned in such a way that

I wanted it removed. The sand, on which I stood, became less supportive and I sank further down. The rest of the world was whizzing by, and life went on, leaving me without the means to be pulled to safety. I waited for my rescue.

I continued to listen to every single solitary word, no matter how much it hurt. It was my belief that if I absorbed, entertained, and considered all things spoken, I would hear the one thing I could hook onto. I was convinced that anything microscopic might be the key to salvation and reconciliation.

When the world slowed down, people began to give advice or offer concrete statements. Once again, I found myself clutching my ears. Opinions hit me like an assault. "What did you do?" "Well, that's ridiculous." "You're the mother." "Have you tried to be honest?" "Did you write them a letter?" "Well, they can't prevent you from seeing your grandchildren." "Maybe you should move away for a while." "Try sending postcards." "Keep buying gifts." "Send texts that don't ask for anything." "Don't ever stop telling them how much you love them."

But what happens when all of these aforementioned efforts produce nothing but more silence? Or more reminders of your inadequacies that suggest your public persona is a fraud? You find yourself waiting for the rest of the world to discover that you are someone who should never leave their house. Because it has been drilled into your head, that eventually, you will stumble. There is no way to keep up the façade of goodness.

Magical thinking sent me on a path of perceived public opinion. "What kind of mother is she when her own children don't want anything to do with her?" It seemed my choice was clear. So, I took my self-worth and flushed it down the toilet. My identity of being a good, kind, and ever-present mother vaporized. Every bit of who I am became particles of dust. Pieces of me whirled in circles before I was sucked down the drain. It was like a long, dark fall off of a very tall cliff. I was given time to contemplate this life before hitting the rocks that battered me to a pulp. But then, I opened my eyes. I was still alive.

So, what does one do with the suggestion to change and be different? My adult life has been an effort to be the best version of who I am. And yet, this is not good enough? I had to stop begging for forgiveness, because this only proved to reveal my incessant need to be the victim. The only cure that was being offered was: "WAKE UP and take responsibility." I'm still not sure of the part I need to own.

I became Alice in Wonderland. I grew quite tall and then quite small, neither of which was right. As I attended the Mad Hatter's tea, a rabbit told me I was late. Quickly I rushed to get to wherever I was supposed to be, only to hear, "Off with her head!" As I swam my ocean of tears, I came to shore and met a Dodo bird. He commanded me and all other estranged parents to run a Caucus race. So, we ran in circles with no beginning and no end. And I finally realized that this nonsensical journey kept delivering me back to the place where I began.

I collected my self-worth and stood upright on my feet. The foundation beneath me is now solid. I am no longer afraid to walk personal truth. My emotional intelligence will not permit me to give anyone permission to define who I am.

Grandparent Alienation

WHAT DOES IT feel like?

(Christine Parsons Photo)

I was screaming at the top of my lungs, "Please don't take away my grandchildren...please give me my family back." Snot and tears were oozing from my facial orifices, as I fell to my knees. And then the phone went dead while I continued to scream. This, I believed, had the power to kill me. I lay there for a while, memories flooding my senses. How to go about reorganizing all the comforts and the patterns we created as a family?

There was a time when I saw my first two grandchildren often. Never going more than two weeks. I cherished the many weekends of having my grandson. His visits felt like dreams come true. He had his own room…the same place his mother slept all those years ago. It seemed a miracle of my motherhood that rewarded me with this precious cherub. On that horrible day that alienated me as a grandparent, I crawled to the door of his little bedroom, and closed it. It felt like a death had occurred. The youth bed, the toys, and the reminders of his physical presence were too painful. All those little rituals we shared were not going to lead to the next. In one lone decision, my family was just gone.

I eventually gave away or stored away anything that reminded me, "I am a grandmother." I bought new paint and new furniture to create a different space. Today, I keep the door open, and we no longer call it, "The Baby's Room."

After the first year, I tried showing up unannounced, thinking my presence would jar us back to reality, hoping that my love would rise to the surface and push away the anger and pain. My granddaughter asked me, "Are you Mommy's friend?" Oh, my precious babe…"Yes, sweetie, I am Mommy's friend." How could I go into a tale of kinship? Especially knowing the other grandmothers were ever present and recognizable. And though, from that day, we continued with a few more visits...the pain and anger remained, and my love sank to the bottom like a stone. With very few words, we fell back into silence.

The father and his wife reside only twenty minutes from me door to door. Facebook would accost me with lives gone on without me. Staring at the computer screen, I tried to catch my breath. There was my family enjoying a BBQ at a nearby lake. My daughters, their husbands, and beautiful cherubs all swimming, laughing, and playing. Though they slept that close to the house they grew up in, not one word passed between us. And they left town in silence. For me, it was like they were never there. But my head told my heart that they had been.

Time has not offered me blurred vision of those images. Though it was years ago, I can still "see" the post of that visit. It is etched in my memory. This requires me to work at keeping those pictures on a shelf that I can't reach. The recollections only exacerbate my grief. I know that my daughters come and go with their families, but I don't need to know the details. Information only offers me a place to sit and ruminate. My poor head whirling with scenarios of magical thinking. I have since blocked social media from all extended families. This was a mindful effort in order to save myself.

But the sad truth is the effort of blocking information won't prevent reality. Though we learn so much about other lives at the touch of a button, we still engage with people face to face.

It was the day after Thanksgiving. We attend an annual event my friend calls "Turkey Busters." Her motivation: "Come and sweat gravy!" And we line up to perform the carefully planned circuit training. It was an unwitting friend who turned to face me. She was jubilant with what she thought was something to celebrate, "Congratulations on becoming a grandmother again!" It felt as though someone had taken their fist and plunged it through my skin, crushing bones to wrench my heart. The news came as an assault, squeezing any semblance of the life I was trying to build. It was a truth beyond my comprehension. One of my daughters had or was having another baby.

I struggled to stay upright as my equilibrium swiftly forced this effort. The room began to spin, and without thought, words just spilled from my lips: "Who had a baby?" This brought instant chaos of incomprehension between two innocent souls. How does the mother not know her child is having a child? Reality filled the space between us. Rapid heartbeats…and a lot of stuttering. Tears rolled from my eyes. They spilled off of my chin and onto my chest. I had to leave the class.

Four months later, my fourth grandchild was born. A friend posted my daughter's blog on Facebook. It announced her baby's birth. It was like an explosion.

Though I grabbed my chair to remain seated, I fell to earth. No matter how fast you may run, news can still catch you.

Information about your own child sounds like a shrill cry that violently hits your eardrums. There is a sudden plummet into darkness. We must recover, and it becomes a quest to climb back into the light. It is a life that sent us on a path unchosen. Our work is to learn how to celebrate what life is, while walking tenderly around what we thought it would be.

Our son has confessed that he avoids Facebook. It's too painful. Life has become an "us and them." In the exact moment when estrangement became the solution, we were no longer one family.

Sometimes when I open my cupboards, and I look at the little Mickey Mouse plate, I can still hear my grandson's voice: "GG, where is my itty-bitty plate, and my itty-bitty spoon? Can I have PBJ toast?" And I would make him breakfast, filling Mickey's ears with apple sauce, while he watched Dumbo over and over again. When he would hear my husband's car come up the driveway in the afternoon, he quickly run outside to greet him. Swooped up in loving arms, his chubby little hands cupping his grandfather's face, "Pop…I am here to visit!! Are you so happy?" The response was always, "Yes, baby, I am so happy."

Letter to My Grandchildren

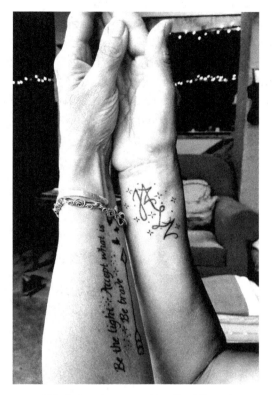

(Christine Parsons Family Album)

Dear J, A, Z, L, & Z

It was never my choice to be absent from your life. Unfortunately, circumstances outside my control prevailed. Please know that I missed you every day. I hope this letter will help you know how much I love you. I will continue to watch over you from wherever I am. You are part of me, and therefore, strong, proud, and bright with an amazing sense of humor. Life will always come down to the ability to laugh...even when things are not that funny. Dance, sing, and be silly. Most importantly, be kind. Know that a life lived without regret is a life filled with purpose.

 GG

Not Enough

(Ariella Neville Photo)

AS AN ESTRANGED parent, I lived to hear the words that expressed my best was not enough. My troubled childhood created all efforts in becoming the mother I wish I had. I remained mindful to avoid presenting myself as a wounded child. I worked every day to keep my past out of my present. I knew that old stuff could retaliate against my future.

My mother was mentally ill. She was not capable of showing up for me. All of my formative years were spent as a witness. She was rarely at peace. Each day found her fighting demons. I represented ground zero.

Though innocent, I was held in contempt for all of her life's misfortune. My childhood was enmeshed in abuse. Survival required me to stay one step ahead.

Her rage went so deep, that my mother committed horrible atrocities, physical and mental. I was never permitted to stray far from her box of expectations. This taught me that any lapse in judgment came with dire consequences.

I came to understand that my mother's perpetual state of chaos had nothing to do with me. And here I am, experiencing adult child estrangement, once again accused of all life's misfortune. My past has taught me that everything can't be my fault.

Each one of us is doing our best with what we know. Knowledge empowers us to do better. But this comes with the passing of each day. Twenty-four hours of lessons that need to be lived in order to gain a higher intelligence. This teaches us how to proceed with tomorrow. Understanding that once something is said or done, it becomes the past. There are no do overs.

My evolution requires me to believe that my parents did do their best. For so long I saw them as inept. It was a temporary fix to shame them for not doing better. No one commits themselves to failure. Our reactions to emotional circumstances are most often provoked by something in our past. We don't know the burden that others carry. So, we are best to meet them where they are.

My responsibility is to use my own experiences to guide my choices. The hope is to proceed in kindness. While it is OK to be mad, it is never OK to be cruel. So how do we shine light on things that are remembered in darkness? By putting emotions into words, and speaking them in a calming tone. Screaming an unrelenting pain avoids the issue and offers no solutions.

Our adult children know they are hurting. It is the definition of WHY they hurt that produces the words to heal. Silence befalls us when we are struck with an inability to express the source of where the pain began. A healing dialogue will can build on these simple words: "I feel this way because...."

The Anatomy of Estrangement

(Christine Parsons Photo)

STAGE 1: APOLOGIZING for every pain your child has ever felt. This is due to the implication that you should have saved them from their own feelings.

Stage 2: Begging and pleading for mercy because their absence is more than you can bear. You are willing to take the blame for everything just to make it stop.

Stage 3: Sending texts, letters, e-mails, and gifts, hoping for a dialogue. You don't care if the communication offers more character assassination. Anything is better than nothing.

Stage 4: The realization, that if you do reach out, you must be prepared to have zero expectation. More often than not, the attempts to engage come with more silence or more expressions of pain and anger.

Stage 5: Blocking all avenues of social media and committing yourself to no more attempt at contact. Seeing lives gone on without you…is much too painful. Having stood on the precipice to the bowels of hell…you will learn the most profound lesson of all: self-care. We cannot heal anyone but ourselves.

Stage 6: Pray for the mind and heart of the adult child, while longing for the answer to, "How long and how far do you want to carry this burden?" Understanding that this is a choice.

Stage 7: Repeat stages 1-6. Healing is not on a linear line. You will experience emotions that spiral in and out of anger, denial, depression, bargaining, and acceptance. Be kind to yourself. Allow the emotions to rise. Your tears are meant to cleanse.

Move On and Let Go

(Christine Parsons Photo)

TRAUMA IS NEVER not trauma. Our painful experiences will not be remembered without suffering. We can heal from our hardships, though we can't forget. It is work to allow them to become part of our story.

It is my belief that there are many things that DON'T happen for a reason. Some of our painful experiences will never make sense. But we can evolve to a place that frees us from hurt and anger. The experiences are stepping stones in the process of getting to higher ground. When pain is given a purpose, it provides a sense of direction. I am best when putting effort into creating light from dark circumstances.

MOVE ON AND LET GO

Estrangement is an ongoing grief. Our child is still alive and having relationships with other people. No one sends cards or drops off casseroles. The general public rarely understands that this experience does resemble a death. But, there is no ceremony where dear friends come to pay condolences. We grieve for all the missed opportunities because of an unwillingness to hash out our differences.

It sounds glib when someone offers, "Maybe it's time to let go." It sounds like a simple solution to complicated matters of the heart. Letting go is an art form. It is a daily mindful practice that will never become a destination. We can reach an acceptance of what is true, but letting go is not an off switch. It is a decision to release all the things that no longer serve you. And there are some days when the sadness must be acknowledged.

I have experienced many days of needing to express my grief and have received empathy in return. I was, understandably, at a low when finding out I had a fifth grandchild. A friend was prattling on about her own grandchildren and the number of new offspring between her and her siblings. This brought me to a breaking point and I firmly stated, "I'm pretty sad after learning that my daughter had her third child." My friend did not pause, and actually sounded a bit angry, "I thought you'd moved on from this. I thought you were finally OK with never seeing your daughters again!!"

This indicated that I should have arrived at a place with all my suitcases and every personal possession. Moving on should find me on the map living down the road from grief. I had this image of receiving news of a new grandchild in the form of water. It should have simply rolled off my back like it would to a duck. But I'm not a duck. So, in the throes of this devastating expectation I quietly responded, "Every bit of news about my daughters instantly becomes an emotional reaction. Once this happens, I have to recover, and this takes time. Yes, I can be OK, but there will never come a time when I don't care."

This journey requires me to keep it real. I work at staying present. It is an effort for me to not rehash every ugly moment. I must be mindful every time I punish myself for having lost my temper. Child rearing is laced with question marks. Did I go too far? Did I say things I wish to take back? Was I frustrated? Was I angry? Were there moments when I wanted to be any other place than in the bosom of my family? Yes, to all. I have to remind myself to release all thoughts that I arrived in this place of estrangement by myself.

Friendships have been compartmentalized. I steer away from expecting the naked woman to give me her shirt. When I am on my game, I can be with people that don't understand my process. And when I am not, I stick with those who can sit with me in my sadness without offering solutions. It is to see the forest for the trees without focusing on that one broken limb.

Emotional Strategy

(Ariella Neville Photo)

EMOTION + LOGIC = Mindfulness. The best strategy is to own and accept responsibility for your own feelings. If we throw logic at high emotion, it will give time for things to simmer. Once we feel rational, we are able to apply a thoughtful approach to conflict.

As estranged parents, we have been on the receiving end of high emotion void of logic. We sit with an implanted seed that we knew better but didn't do better. All past emotions of discomfort correlate with an event. It is believed that we should have protected our children. I have been told that I simply chose not to show up.

The verbal purging insinuates that we are responsible. The inability to let go is our fault. It's as though we possess an invisible force to all things conflicting. It's comforting to hold on to what we know to be true. There is truth in our past because it can't be changed. The future seems riddled with uncertainty. Moving forward requires us to visit past experiences. There are lessons in the way it was done. It is the acknowledgement of the places where we stumbled that can guide us to creating change for the better.

The sad truth is we cannot heal other people...not even our own children. This is not a scraped knee, and there is no Band Aid for internal struggle when it's not our own.

Nobody wakes up in the morning thinking, " I want to F**K this whole thing up." Angry and indignant as we may become, it is the behavior we hate... not the people. If we turn around and say, "They are not doing their best," we have joined in the game.

We are all in constant contemplation of our own emotional strategy. Each one of us wants to be as peaceful as possible. And so, it is for our children. They are doing their best. And as painful as this truth might be, we can alleviate some of our own struggle by meeting them where they are. People can't give us what they don't have.

There are moments when we become so angry

over the loss that it feels like hatred. And we believe our children feel the same toward us. But neither is true. It is the love that keeps us hopeful. And it is the love that keeps our estranged children justifying the pain they believe we caused. In some ways, they are waiting for their rescue.... holding on to a belief that it will be a quick fix to these complicated circumstances.

Past trauma needs to find the words. For now, we can put the hate on the game but not on the player. It is vital that we remain steadfast to self-care. Nourish your brain with kindness, and free yourself of anger. This will prepare you for the slightest whisper of reconciliation. I wish you peace.

STRATEGY

? Or to lves?

(Christine Parsons Photo)

WHENEVER I AM in a state of unrest with someone I love, it becomes all- consuming. My mind rarely leaves the dialogue that will speak my emotions. I begin with thoughts of self-righteousness, because I have been unduly wronged. As I work it out in my head, I realize that "right" fighting will not yield better results. My emotions simmer and logic creeps in. Conflict resolution needs a discussion of the issues that caused the emotion.

UNTO US? OR TO THEMSELVES?

I try to imagine living with the weight and gravity of this chaos. I envision a struggle of lugging it along like a beast of burden. Yet, stubborn in my own truth, I refuse to take the outstretched hand that offers a release from this conflict. Instead, my choice is silence. A silence that turns into another day, month, and perhaps even years. I think to myself, "How must it feel to give anger all that attention as a daily practice?" Because even if I would try to be happy, the crippling turmoil would be the undercurrent in everything I do. And without a choice, unresolved conflict becomes behavior.

As estranged parents, we see our circumstances as being done to us. Now try to hold a beach ball under water for an indefinite period of time. It is to put all effort into keeping the issues submerged. A mighty truth keeps fighting back, and pushes to reach the surface. Wouldn't that be exhausting? Though happiness might come in waves, there is no opportunity to rest. The beach ball requires daily service, and everything else becomes secondary to this task.

The silence feels that this it is being done to us. We wish for the opportunity to "right" fight our own truth. Even though this is void of logic, our thinking is distorted by our feelings of being so deeply hurt. And though it seems that our adult children have just gone on their merry way...they are hurting too. Their silence is born out of fear.

There was something my son said to me that gave

me clarity to our circumstances. "If I was so mad that I stopped talking to you, it would be all I could think about all day every day." This caused me to remember one of the last things I spoke to my daughter. I asked, "Don't you miss having me in your life?" She said, "No," and continued, "If I don't see you, I don't have to think about this." But there was exhaustion in her tone, and I was keenly aware of the beach ball she is working to keep submerged. My sadness is knowing that she is not yet ready to set the truth free.

Common Denominator?

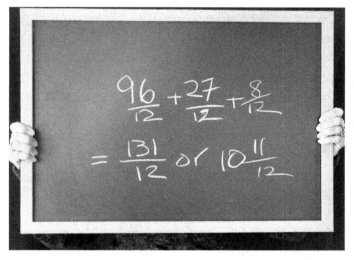

(Ariella Neville Photo)

I AM ABLE to date my family's history with estrangement all the way back to the 1800s. The history includes money, marriage, divorce, jealousy, and non-productive accusations. Anger always begins with pain. People fall silent when they don't know how to express their emotions. Talking about feelings, for many, is a sign of weakness. I find to the contrary. Emotional intelligence is the most powerful wisdom of all.

We are privy to what seems an epidemic of family issues due to social media. Thirty years ago, we would never know how many families suffer in fragments. Both of my parents took their silence to the grave, leaving unresolved conflict as a legacy. Their extended families are strangers to me, as we never had the opportunity to forge any type of bond or relationship.

The estrangement with my own children is born of a need to see one parent as all good. The emotional damage this has caused hides in the shadows. We fall silent because it feels like the best solution. If we don't talk about it, it's not there, and it can't get worse.

I can put together many reasons to blame. But this is something that causes me to steer clear. Creating an identity of who is at fault doesn't change a thing. We are adults making a collection of choices. Handing over the responsibility of wrong doing to one person is not productive.

Estrangement will find its way into any socioeconomic race, creed, or religion. The common denominator is being human. Hurt people hurt people. Some of us will use pain in an effort to create a purpose. And others won't. I find I am better when I'm not bitter. There is a process that this experience has taught me before I speak: Is it true? Is it necessary? Is it kind?

Hit From Behind

(Ariella Neville Photo)

AS MUCH AS I would like to call acceptance a destination, I still have those days of being an emotional wreck. I can be triggered by a song, a smell, or just hearing someone prattle on about their grandchild. Emotions hit me without notice, and it feels like a sudden blow to the back of the head. Tears burn in my eyes, and I fight through the overwhelming despair that will put me to bed. These are times when I go to my own written words for comfort and reminders. It is a necessary effort to keep a forward march.

My spiritual journey through this estrangement is

a maze of choices. There are clusters of intersections that never offer an obvious straight line. All the emotions seem familiar. They just look different the farther down the road I travel. I wish I could just arrive and unpack my bags. So, the days of feeling any kind of acceptance are greeted with exuberance. My days of sadness still come, no matter how much I wish them away. I miss my family. Or rather, I am left to imagine the family that I thought we would be.

My heart and my mind allow me these days of lapsing into the abyss. This is done, with the understanding that I shall not dwell in this space. While it is OK to be sad, it is never OK to be incapacitated. I make sure that I don't become comfortable in the darkness. Sometimes it is tempting to call in an interior decorator to make this space more appealing. Inevitably, I call my posse and circle the wagons. I surround myself with beautiful things. I stick with the people who greet me with sincerity. This has created a weeding of the herd, and a process of rewriting my address book. I don't need solutions. I just need empathy.

Saved From Drowning

(Christine Parsons Photo)

ESTRANGED PARENTS MOURN for people who are still alive. And so, we cycle through and around the stages of grief. The quest to reach acceptance becomes a daily practice. There are good days and bad. Slowly we arrive at a place where we accept reality. This doesn't mean we have to say, "It's OK."

Our children are trapped inside their anger, using silence as a weapon. This comes without cause for solutions. Healing begins with a willingness to address the hard issues. By revealing the truth, the anger can be set free. We are all accountable in what went wrong. It is the definition of what part we need to own that remains in question.

We have heard so many times, "You made me feel..." when we have no control over other people's emotions. A simple twist that offers a different perspective is why the feelings happened. Not who.

Our adult children remember their past as surviving years of neglect. A reality that we stood idly by without lifting a finger in prevention of devastating conclusions. It's as if we just watched them drown while sitting comfortably in a lounge chair. Turning our head while their arms and legs were flailing to stay afloat. An image of us putting in our ear buds to mute the high-pitched screaming that begged to be saved. An implication that their cries for help were in vain. We just didn't pay attention. So, they sank like a stone. Someone else had to jump in and pull them to safety. And we are left to wonder where all those parental moments of love and nurture went.

These truths put us in a place with no line of defense. It becomes a battle that cannot be won. Everyone is holding steadfast to their truth. I have learned to be empathetic to all the perceived realities. I do this while holding steadfast to my own. It is prudent for me to move away from anger, as I am better when I feel calm.

Stirring the Pot

(Ariella Neville Photo)

PEOPLE OFTEN SAY what makes them feel better. They offer quick solutions to complicated matters. "Oh, they'll come around." Or "They just need to mature." This leaves us with the notion that we just need to be patient. But for some of us, this has been years of waiting. All the while, each day is met with the challenge of navigating the truth. I don't have a relationship with my daughters or their children.

Patience does not remove the ache in my heart. Estrangement requires a mindset of bravery. Keeping the door open to opportunity. Summoning up the strength to keep our heads out of the past. Taking every opportunity to celebrate all the blessings that surround us every day.

I get it. Most people just want us to be free of the pain. Sometimes their efforts resemble anger and exasperation. I have had friendships end for the sole reason of being sick and tired of my ongoing grief. It's a difficult comprehension for those who don't walk this path. Compassion gets worn down through a perception that we are holding onto to something that should be let go. There might come suggestions that we look at estrangement like an amputation. A simple process of coming to terms with the missing limb.

As estranged parents, we see our situation as being done to us. But with closer examination, our children are also doing this to themselves. They must wake each day by renewing the anger that keeps them silent. I think of it as a bubbling cauldron that needs constant stirring. Due diligence to ensure that nothing sticks to the bottom. I imagine myself sleeping at night with spoon in hand. Getting out of bed with each sunrise, and going back to the pot. There are no days off.

Our children believe that we inflicted their pain. They cannot clearly see the release button that will free them of this conflict. It is just one mindful decision to let go of the spoon. While we love them and want to heal their discomfort, it is not up to us to soothe all the unsettling emotions. Their healing can only come from the inside out. And so, we wait and we hope that they will come find us in the place where we have been all along. Home with open arms.

Imagine

(Christine Parsons Family Album)

IMAGINE THE ESTRANGED child is stuck in fear. The belief that one or both of their parents must be

removed. It becomes necessary to cut us out like a cancer in order to save them from further harm. The result of their hurled accusations gains a temporary relief. It is an experience that feels, initially, peaceful, but doomed to crash. Sadly, we are bound to fall right back to where we started. And the cycle repeats. The conflict rises, and the pain remains. Blame is sent out in one direction without pause to see the collective effort. We arrived here together.

Imagine the ability to soothe the discomfort. Slowly releasing the burden of our children's emotional conflict. We have come to believe we are being punished for perceived wrong doing. We have spewed and babbled apologies. We have thrown ourselves at their feet. We have tried to create a defense against a reality that differs from our own.

Imagine if we were able to erase the accusations. Simply wash away the attempts that were made to set us up to fail. If only we could remove their doubts, and eradicate all fear, anxiety, abandonment, and sadness. Go after the past with a sledge hammer to demolish their beliefs that have become concrete.

Imagine having the power to stop our children from feeling their own emotions. They finally recognize our set of loving arms and listening ears. Gaining in our telepathy to impose our will. At long last, peeling that onion so we might meet the truth.

Imagine your adult child sleeping on a pillow of internal conflict. The clock is ticking as every day is met with a defiant truth. How much time will pass? Emotional unrest becomes behavior. And we are made to watch this from a distance.

Imagine your adult child offers permission to work the problem. They agree to practice forgiveness. They have arrived at a final destination to a place that releases them from all the things that no longer serves them. It is an onset of awareness that gives them an unweighted freedom. An experience of being lighter than air.

Imagine your child is a helium balloon. The give voice to the breeze that will carry them home. Flying through the clouds to be greeted by loving arms.

Imagine there is always hope. Remain diligent in self-care. This is not your fault.

When the Mourning Doesn't End

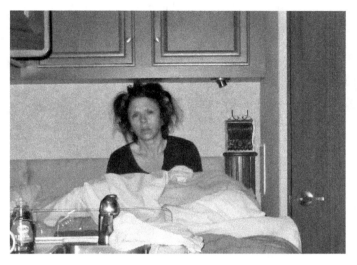

(Christine Parsons Family Album)

I HAVE REALIZED that I am always on the edge of a place that will remind me of loss. Some dear unsuspecting soul is around a corner and bound to share news of my daughters and their families.

Unsolicited information that throws me head-first into the deep end of the pool. I am standing at the bottom looking up. The sky is in full view, but my arms won't move. Sound is muffled, as my heart begs to be free from the words that spill out like poison. Information.

Sometimes, if I am in a place of strength, I can command an answer to, "How are your grandchildren?" or "What are your daughters up to these days?" I can be OK for a bit. But, the reminder of loss plants a seed. Inevitably, emotions rise and they have to come out somewhere, someplace, sometime. They always do.

Today I grapple with the sadness that feels destined. My daughters and their children don't come anymore. This is where I sit with my level of acceptance. Weaving in and out of bargaining, and denial. Today I mourn.

To Peanut

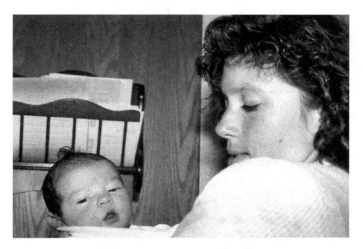

(Christine Parsons Family Album)

A MOTHER'S HEART holds many compartments. A mother's heart has the capacity to fill emptiness and abate fear. A mother's heart has love enough to surround all doubts. A mother's heart does not discriminate.

The path of your life has given you cherished memories filled with beautiful people. You will grow and flourish by each recollection of every precious moment. You will grow and flourish by each recollection of every pain and sorrow.

We learn in everything we do. Good or bad. Therefore, we must always pay attention, learning to say thank you in the face of adversity. For there is another opportunity to grow.

Every morning that you wake, be grateful for the day. Always be thankful for what you have. Be happy for others in their own accomplishments. It is those, with a kind spirit who attract generosity. Jealousy breeds more of the same.

Find beauty in all the little things. Don't wait for moments of grandeur. They will come few and far between. The little things will constantly surround you.

Always remember: A life lived without regret is a life full of purpose.

I was asked by my daughter's sorority sisters to compose reflections of a mother's love and pride. A gathering would be held as graduation day approached. The letters and photos would be shared during a celebration of sisterhood. This came four years into our first estrangement. I had to summon up the courage to complete this task free of my own anger and pain. It took three months and so many buckets of tears. To do this correctly, I had to write void of despair. How could I have known that estrangement would remain in her heart, as the safe place to live. And I am silenced for the third time. My dear little peanut....

Grandchildren

(Christine Parsons Family Album)

I BELIEVED THAT becoming a grandparent was a gift. It was the reward for every hard decision I had to make as a parent. It was seamless, the immersion into this role that only required a deep sense of love. I threw myself in with free abandon. I dove head first without fear. I never could have imagined that, like a rug, this relationship would be pulled away...and ripped from beneath my feet.

This left me face down on the floor. It took a long time for me to get back up. Like an infant, I had to learn how to crawl, walk, and eventually run. Running far away from the darkness. Life marched on, and there was a task at hand: the mission to keep living. So, I grabbed hold of anything or anyone that aided me in my quest to release the overwhelming shame and doubt.

My face peered into the light, and my body would soon follow. Slowly I began to learn how to celebrate every blessing no matter how small. There are still moments when I continue to grieve for the time that feels lost. And then I remind myself to keep looking forward. All will be revealed. This absence was never my choice. I have been here all along...with arms open wide.

Who Holds Your Hand?

(Christine Parsons Photo)

A FRIEND POSTED a story which represented the grief of loss. It was a reminder to live each day as though it is your last. A nudge to relish the time spent with the people we care about. The moral in the end is to love deeply and selflessly.

When your own children choose to estrange, it is a loss that a parent grieves. I always believed that I loved deeply and selflessly...and then I was told that I didn't. Handed that belief, I began to adopt it as true. I had no idea who I was anymore.

As I fell hard and fast down the rabbit hole, my

husband gently reminded me of the blessings that are right in front of me. There were many, and I allowed it to penetrate. With each breath, my heart acknowledged each dear soul who became my posse. Whenever I doubt how I love, I need only remind myself how to receive. Everything we give will come back to us.

Grief reorganizes the way we think and the commitment to how we feel about others. And perhaps we wonder how others feel about us. With each loss, there comes a greater devotion to those who show up. They are my definition of family. These are the people who will hold my hand when I need it most.

Tears That Cleanse

(Christine Parsons Photo)

SOMETIMES WE TELL ourselves to "Let Go" or "Move On." We grow weary of feeling the emotions, and shedding the tears. Though it is all part of this process, it is exhausting. And sometimes those around us become exhausted by our feelings.

I haven't seen my daughters since 2016. They visit the father, just one town over, coming and going without notice to me. Sometimes people are excited to tell me, "I met your daughter and your grandchildren!" And so, comes that horrible pit in my stomach that speaks my vulnerability to how I answer.

I have to wrack my brain to come up with an appropriate response. It takes great effort to override the nagging thoughts that tell me I should have let go or moved on by now. Believe me, my body wishes it was in a different place with a brighter view.

So yes, I still cry. My tears cleanse the ache in my heart, and allow me to proceed with greater emotional intelligence. I never wanted estrangement, and it is, therefore, not mine to fix. While I stay within this reality, I continue to pray for light to shine in dark places. I count all the tiny miracles that are realized because of this experience. Thankful for understanding that this life offers an abundance of all things that are priceless.

To Be Seen for Who You Are

(Christine Parsons Family Album)

WHEN ESTRANGEMENT BEGAN to brew, I realized how much I was defending myself. I kept fighting against scenarios that didn't feel true. Showing up for battles I could never win. I thought it was a noble cause, no matter how bloody my return from the front line. I had to protect myself against the accusations that called me out as a monster.

Slowly I began to realize my overwhelming losses. There was nothing left to do but believe what was being said. I found myself stuttering out incessant apologies, even when I didn't understand the accusations. I became a puddle of weakness as my whole world started to circle the drain.

The cyclone was taking my family, and it felt as though they were being ripped from my arms. I fought for solid ground, but found I was no match against this unrelenting force. I was pulled off my feet and sucked into the long dark funnel. The conclusion had been reached. My efforts were fruitless. I was fighting against air with a pitch-fork. Nothing I said made any difference. Though my actions came from loving kindness, the funnel of darkness stretched out before me. There was not a glimmer of light.

I kept going to the mirror, hoping to see my unwavering love. And for a long time, the reflection presented me as a three-headed beast. Self-doubt, guilt, and shame consumed me in recounting my every moment of anger and frustration. Motherhood was so complicated. I tried to soothe my soul with the notion that I really did do my best. But sadly, I was set on a journey of shoulda, woulda, coulda. All effort became a mindset to reconstruct the past.

My husband and son took to busying themselves by walking behind me to clean up the carnage. They never tried to fix me as I shattered into tiny pieces. Instead, they allowed me to grieve. They commanded a presence of broad shoulders and listening ears. And so, it was with amazing grace, that I found the courage to put myself back together.

Estrangement finds me here in this moment. I look in the mirror and see myself, warts and all. I am so beautifully flawed. Every crack and chink in my armor represents the warrior princess that lives inside my heart.

I am not weak. Talking about emotions and identifying why they surface has become my super power. I walk this journey by my own definition. I am a person of value. Please see me for who I am, without wishing I was somebody else.

Walking a Path Unchosen

(Christine Parsons Photo)

WHEN SILENCE FIRST fell between me and my adult daughters, it was like high tide. The sand was slipping away from beneath my feet. "Someone please, throw me a life line. I am falling into the abyss." My experience found me realizing the unimaginable. The feelings of isolation, so profound, I thought I was living in an alternate universe. Nothing seemed familiar so I began searching. My quest was to find anything that I could grab hold of. Though it was a relief, I was deeply saddened to find a large community of parents just like me. There were too many to count. All of them could relate to this notion of shame, embarrassment, guilt, and whatever negative feelings rise on a daily basis. Are we all getting what we deserve?

The older I get, the more I understand how fragile relationships really can be. They hang on every word, and at times, become messy and complicated. I use my past whenever I feel the gravity of a decision. It is why I begged, "We need to talk more, not less." This silence has no potential to move us forward.

I sit with almost two decades of collective effort with my daughters. This journey has taught me to dig deep and study hard for reasonable answers. Immersing myself in what is really being said. What I have heard is pain that is not mine to own.

When faced with the sounds of silence, our brain tricks us into believing that a harmful dialogue is better than no dialogue at all. For me, I can't bear to hear another word that attempts to strip me of my worth.

The evolution of estrangement has been a lesson of meeting people where they are. All attempts are to present myself with compassion. Every once in a while, I will knock on the door that leads to the passage of healing. If I had the key, I would just let myself in. Sadly, I look up at the looming tower where my daughters live. They have built a structure around their hearts, and it appears as an impenetrable fortress. They have created a safe place from conflicting emotions. I understand the fear of opening the door. For them, it is a risk that will cause greater harm. They see me as the Trojan horse.

In-as-much as their silence keeps them safe, strangely, the silence offers me the same. I, too, am relieved of any further harm. And this is the very reason the fortress should have been dismantled a long time ago. Now, we are all making decisions based on fear. The greater the amount of time that goes in between, the greater the reality of magical thinking, and the potential to ruminate over things that are not true.

I recognize how we all make choices based on where we place the most value. I grapple with the valued choice that requires my daughters to leave me behind. My work is a journey to allow; to receive; to accept; to admit; to adopt; to agree. I take advantage of the stillness that offers me the pursuit of self-care. I place value on productive words: "We need to talk more, not less."

We walk a path unchosen. The journey is so deeply personal. We all stand in different places, though we are working the same circumstances. There is no map or right way to go about this. It is a destination of uncertainty, yet, hope remains. Replace fear with love.

Tell the Universe

(Christine Parsons Photo)

I TOLD THE universe, "This is not what I signed up for." And the reply, "Pay attention."

Sometimes we are handed challenges that seem too difficult to bear. We ride the roller coaster of emotions, holding on with both hands, with the fear of falling.

Emotional intelligence allows us to take on adversity from a place of strength. If it were up to us, estrangement would have never been a solution. That choice was made for us. So, when the universe signs you up for a course of life lessons, pay attention. Everything that challenges you becomes your teacher.

May yesterday's wisdom grace you with the beauty of today.

Don't Take the Bait

(Christine Parsons Family Album)

ESTRANGEMENT HAS TAUGHT me the true meaning of fair fighting. My go-to phrase: "It is OK to be mad. It is never OK to be cruel." When we choose to engage, careful consideration should be given to the words we speak. A simple arrangement of expression can significantly alter the outcome. If we give thought to the desired result, we stay focused on the end game. Ask yourself, "How do I want people to feel when I turn to walk away? Better, worse, or the same?"

When emotions run high, we are apt to dole out knee-jerk reactions. This provokes examination after the fact. "Why did I say that?" It becomes a brain exercise to hit the pause button, subsequently, dimming that propensity to right fight. Though we have grown weary of silence, it can also be used as a powerful tool of engagement. We don't need to show up for every fight.

Retaliating against hurtful dialogue creates more harm. Don't take the bait. The people that love us most know every button to push. They are begging for a reaction. But if you calmly respond, or say nothing at all, where can the argument go?

There are times when we are embroiled in an argument we can't win. A quiet hand gesture can speak a whole sentence. The above photo is my teenage response to conflicting feelings of total exasperation: "No. Are you really taking my picture right now?!" Today I am a little wiser and suggest no hand gesture at all.

Fair fighting has rules: Stay calm; no accusations; no hitting below the belt; avoid words like "always" and "never."

Allow emotions to simmer as the logic equalizes

in your brain. This will bring you to a place of calm. Our words are more accurate when our mind is at peace. Keep your wits about you. Smiling will put out a fire faster than you think.

No Matter Where You Go, You Bring Yourself

(Christine Parsons Photo)

A FRIEND OF mine grew frustrated with my ongoing challenges of estrangement. I had recently been gob smacked with information about my daughter. I felt safe sharing my sadness. Her reaction spun me in circles. "Can't you just move away for a year or so?" My guardian angel summoned up the most appropriate response: "There is no geographical location that will free me of my grief."

No matter where we go, we bring ourselves. The

scenery is determined by where we stand emotionally and physically. I have learned that the quest for happiness is a destination. Once there we are searching for that next great thing. But if we choose to live in joy, it becomes a lifestyle. This mindset promotes self-care.

Yes, there will be good days and bad. But we have the power to give ourselves what others don't have to give. Be the change you wish to see. The search begins inside your own heart.

When Expectation Finds Reality

(Christine Parsons Photo)

POWERFUL TRUTHS:

The naked man can't give you his shirt.

Stop waiting for the cat to bark.

Don't try to get water from an empty well.

Most people don't see their beliefs. Instead, their beliefs tell them what to see. This is the simple difference between clarity and confusion.

I Grieve

THIS WILL RESONATE for those who miss their innocent babes.

(Christine Parsons Photo)

My arms swing furiously
At what I thought was there.
My heart beats quickly
As silence is despair.

A disconnected mother knows
Little what to do.
My love is lost in space
And words have become few.

NEVERTHELESS THEY PERSISTED

No matter what I say,
The vitriol rapid-fires.
This was never my choice
But it is sadly their desire.

I learn to celebrate life.
It is mine and clear to take.
It is not what I expected
But never seen as a mistake.

In the meantime, kiss the foreheads
Of the babes I miss so much.
GG's heart will remain forever
Imagining their touch.

I hope I am not gone
Just soon to be found again.
My prayers will not stop
In hopes to see you when.

I grieve and allow in sadness.
And proceed wiser than before.
I wish for new beginnings
Closing this chapter
To an opening door.

The Estranged Parent and Alienated Grandparent Often Feel They Are Walking...The Yellow Brick Road

(Ariella Neville Photo)

I HAVE FELT like Dorothy, swept away on the winds of a tornado. I believed that my journey was to discover OZ, meet the all and powerful wizard, and joyfully be sent back to where I belong.

I told everyone I met, "There is no place like home." And I tried to do everything right to get there. My heart ached to be back in the bosom of my family. Despite feelings of losing pieces of who I am, I stayed on the Yellow Brick Road. There were dark moments that seemed, the harder I tried, the farther away I became.

I awoke in a field of poppies. OZ stood tall and glorious on the horizon. A whisper in my ear told me, I was "finally taking steps in the right direction." The notion of OZ was dream like. I ran toward the magnificent gates, only to be told, once there, that I had no access.

The wizard flew away without me, and I was left in this place unfamiliar. Though I had traveled so far, I was no closer than when I started.

Weary, I began to blink my eyes. I struggled to see. The dust from the tornado was settling, and a realization was taking hold. I was in my own bed. As it turns out, OZ was not a place or a destination. It has always been the truth inside my heart.

No one can tell us the things in life that are priceless. It is a continuous journey of discovery. Every day, we make choices based on where we place the most value. The hope is to have little regret.

Personal truth does not live somewhere over the rainbow. Dreams realized are no further than our own backyard. There is no place like home. It is where I have been all along.

Preserving the Open Wound

(Ariella Neville Photo)

PAIN AND FEAR are the foundation for anger. We get hurt...and then we get mad. The choice of what to do with these emotions is crucial to the way we resolve conflict. We can blame someone for the way we feel, or we can own it. Because even with an apology, the experience doesn't wash away. We are accountable for soothing our own emotional discomfort.

The past has the potential to rule the present and determine the future. Gone unresolved, it remains an open wound. Each day is spent lugging along that weight of inner turmoil. It provides ammunition for the next episode of shame and blame. Accusations fly based on the feelings and not the actual event.

It appears unpleasant to meet conflict head on. It feels like bringing our dirty laundry out in the open. But if you think of conflict as your friend, you will carve out time to get together. A process of untangling a ball of yarn so we are able to knit a sweater that fits. There is no greater feeling than being unweighted from anger. The effort to reconcile can offer new perspectives. It can lead to compassion and a deeper understanding of another person. Together we might realize what drives our choices.

The alternative is to move the elephant into the living room. We quietly tiptoe about in order to avoid unpleasantness. Maybe things are better left unsaid. But this only creates deeper wounds, and the elephant gets angrier. Ignoring the conflict makes everything worse.

Think of asking this grey mammal, "How did you get into our house? Please tell me what my family needs to do to get you out once and for all." All the answers can move us forward so we can free up space for things more joyful.

We all have a tendency to "revisit" old stuff. It is my belief that our history holds chapters that require attention. When we take the time to soothe old trauma, we are allowing it to become part of our story. To the contrary, the effort placed on keeping past trauma submerged meets a persistent force. It won't stop

PRESERVING THE OPEN WOUND

pushing back. It needs to reach the surface. Without breathing open air, it becomes the behavior.

There is no denying that our hardships knock us down. The challenges of life are sometimes met with, "Why me?" But if we learn to face adversity from a place of strength, the question becomes, "Why not me?" This is when we meet our challenges head on and they become our teacher. The lessons will tell the story of how we got back up.

The process of resolution requires us to identify the event that caused the emotions. Healing those open wounds by asking "What (not who) caused you to feel abandoned, fear, loneliness, doubt, etc." The productive answer starts when we all take responsibility for the way we feel.

There is no need to search for blame. This deafening silence begs for solutions. Sometimes the quiet rings in our ears. And so, we wait. In the meantime, there will be moments of anger and resentment. We are human, after all. But we are best when we are calm. Find purpose. Be brave. Peaceful minds make peaceful choices.

Save Yourself

(Ariella Neville Photo)

MY THERAPIST BEGGED me to stop. Stop all the desperate pleas that begged my daughters to hear my voice. Cease and desist with mindful alternatives that might create solutions. I imagine it was quite difficult to watch me slowly wither away. My community witnessed estrangement as it took every bit of who I am. The underlying fear was that I would become a hollow shell.

I continued to dole out my love long after I became exhausted. I offered a constant reassurance that I really am who I say I am. I incessantly apologized for any bit of pain and discomfort. It was my burden to take, or so I thought. It was in desperation; this need of mine to end the suffering. Alas, the estrangement continues, and with it the perception that this is not fixable. It feels like a life sentence without the chance of parole.

It took me a long while to find the key that released me of these imposed bars. I realized that this prison was of my own design. I had choices, too.

My advice to estranged parents is always to do what feels right to you. Far be it for anyone to tell you this journey has a set of rules. But, If the decision is made to reach out, my suggestion is to be in a place of little expectation. I have found that the accumulation of unresolved conflict keeps generating chaos. It reacts with blame or nothing at all. When we offer generosity and kindness, rarely will it be met with compassion. We try so hard to pour out love, but like water off a duck's back, it just rolls away. Anger becomes an impenetrable force.

I pray that you realize your worth. Build confidence and believe that you never need to defend yourself. Steer clear of those who need to be convinced. There is great comfort in being with people who greet you with sincerity. Find the dear souls who are free of judgment. Bind yourself to a community who cheers for your strengths, and walks tenderly around your weaknesses.

My silence doesn't mean that I left. I concentrate

on the effort to soothe my own soul. Whenever my family chooses to begin the uncomfortable conversations, I will be nourished by my effort to self-care. Each decision, yet to be made, will determine our fate. I never wanted this and finally understand it is not mine to fix.

Desperation

(Ariella Neville Photo)

I REMEMBER SAYING, "If you put me in desperate circumstances, I will start acting desperate." I found myself repeatedly baited into having extreme emotional reactions. And then, to my dismay, everyone would observe my response without any acknowledgement of the cause. Insinuations that my public persona is not genuine. Any actions of kindness or generosity implicates me as a fraud.

It has been suggested that I am a failure at motherhood. If I am acting in accordance with social norms, it's a fluke. "You write a bunch of flowery s**t on social media, and it's not even who you are!" Inevitably, something inside my head snaps like a dry twig. The litany of defense pours out of me as I beg to hold onto my dignity. Time would unearth the stories of how I freaked out for no apparent reason. "What's wrong with her?" And the sympathetic eyes would gaze upon my offspring.

We find ourselves begging and pleading for a reprieve. But the weaker we become; the more power is shifted. I think to myself, "I should just give them the keys to a steam roller. Hand over all my power and allow them to flatten me like a pancake." My weakness proves to perpetuate the accusation that I always play the victim.

Part of my process is the realization that I can't control what people say about me. There is no purpose to defending myself. Blubbering to protect my honor sounds like, "Thou dost protest too much, methinks." I no longer attempt to convince anyone of my worth. The haters are gonna hate.

I have learned to remain silent in the face of accusations. Arguments need at least two people. It is a brain exercise to resist engagement. I grew up in a house believing that the one who screamed the loudest won. But just because it's loud doesn't make it true.

Whatever is yet to unfold in the future will be met with greater emotional intelligence. Be better, not bitter.

The Muddy Puddle

(Ariella Neville Photo)

WHEN WE ARE in the throes of struggle, we search for others who share a common thread. We grab hold of anything that might help us make sense of the unimaginable. I hear many times that adult child estrangement is new. This upcoming generation is spoiled and entitled. But as a product of estrangement, my upbringing aligned me with family who would rather burn it down than confront the issues. Taking silence to the grave was the easiest alternative.

People get pissed off and they stop speaking to each other. If the right words remain unspoken, conflict continues. The more the silence, the worse it gets. Now everyone is basing truth on assumptions and hearsay. Second-hand news becomes fact. This kind of conflict is not bound to any generation or time. Estrangement is the human factor.

Hurt feelings quickly ignites an instinct to kill or be killed. If there are no tools in the tool box, fixing it becomes a major challenge. The issues get blurred, and everyone is screaming pain. Shame and blame get thrown around, and we enter the realm of hitting below the belt. Assigning fault becomes the objective. All sentences begin with, "You..." which ensures the chaos will remain.

I don't feel that estrangement is new or an epidemic. Social media allows us insight to the lives of a mass population. No one talked about estrangement decades ago. No one dared to air their grievances in public. Unpleasant family matters were kept behind closed doors.

More times than not, feelings become facts. These emotions turn into events with a dialogue. An altered reality blossoms, and we fight our own truth. Pain creates more pain, and the arguments are void of logic.

Silence proves to create a larger burden. It grows and weighs heavily on the heart and mind. The decision to estrange is not peaceful. Turmoil whirls like a Dervish in all the things left unsaid. The claim is irreconcilable differences without an effort to reconcile. And we fall further into darkness. I dream and

THE MUDDY PUDDLE

continue to hope for the day when my family becomes breathless and exhausted on the search for solutions.

Estrangement is like a puddle. Every time conflict rises, someone jumps in to stir up all the dirt that quietly rests at the bottom. The clear, standing water is now obstructed by many tiny floating particles. And we wait for everything to settle, believing that once the puddle is clear again, peace will be restored. But the collection of combined will keeps us ready with our boots by the door. With the snap of fingers, we are running toward the puddle, jumping in with both feet, and churning up all that old stuff from the bottom. Sadly, this cycle will keep repeating.

Past hurt will drive our behavior. In disgust we might easily judge, "What's wrong with you?" When we gain in greater emotional intelligence, a simple play on words changes from judgement to concern: "What happened to you?" There is trauma in everyone's history. It deserves attention. These conversations will allow us to store away our boots, only to be used on rainy days. Finally, we can walk past the muddy puddle, and leave it alone once and for all.

Change

(Ariella Neville Photo)

CHANGE! THE SUGGESTION that my state of being is not good enough. Given the silence, this demand seems a paradox. How on earth will anyone know if change has occurred? How will I ever be the same? None of us are who we were five minutes ago. Time guarantees that change is imminent.

As estranged parents, we pray for change. Change in our circumstances. The day when things will be different. We hope for a wiggle of communication. A tidbit of information. We find our curiosity can get the best of us. Wanting to know what's around the next corner. But sometimes the change we seek is not for the better.

That wiggle, that tidbit of news, can find a self-deprecating tragedy. Movement that propels us toward earth. Information that feels like being pushed off a cliff. A free fall destined to hit bottom. Change becomes something to avoid.

There are things that I wish to unknow. Tired in my effort to constantly recover. A yearning to go back to a space of ignorance. And the quandary continues. I am still eager to know what happens next, but with my hands firmly planted over my eyes.

Change is a multi-faceted word. It has the power to exacerbate grief. It's easier for me to believe that nothing changes. Because every new reality begins the emotional process of coming to terms. I just want to hear of my family from the mouths of my family.

Change. It has required me to evolve through this checklist:

Stage One: Simmer the emotions that make me feel like I am on fire.

Stage Two: Crawl back to my personal truth. Make sure to be with people who don't need to be convinced. See the forest for the trees without focusing on one broken limb. Remind myself to celebrate the life I have been given while walking tenderly around the life I thought I would have.

Stage Three: Acceptance. Never to say the circumstances of change are OK. Just being honest with what has become reality. All the while repeating: I am a good, kind, and loving parent, grandparent, partner, and friend.

Stage Four: Repeat stages one through three.

I recently received news that I have a new grandson. Right now, I am shattered china strewn across the cement floor. Operating today based on Stage One. Tomorrow will begin the process of putting myself back together. All the pieces of who I am are glued back together with fine strands of gold. The perfect piece of china now indicates all the cracks and crevices that represent my life experience. Perhaps not perfect, but still, something magnificent. Our imperfections reveal the ways we are so beautifully flawed.

Shoulda, Woulda, Coulda

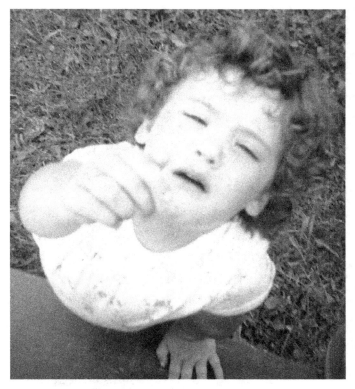

(Christine Parsons Photo)

ALL TOO OFTEN, sentences are used with: shoulda, woulda, coulda. These are words that put all effort into reconstructing a memory. Reality is the ultimate truth finder. It tells us that the second we act and react, it's already in the past. There is no going back.

Day of the Robe

(Ariella Neville Photo)

MY SPIRITUAL JOURNEY through adversity is a maze of choices. There are clusters of intersections that are never an obvious straight line. All the emotions are familiar. They just feel a little different the further down the road I travel. I wish I could just arrive at a destination and call it good. My days of acceptance are glorious. My days of sadness still come no matter how much I wish them away.

I call my days of grief a "Day of the Robe." It is a phrase that has stuck with me for many years. A friend of mine lived in San Francisco, with a very flamboyant roommate. She arrived home one day to find him on the couch. He was scantily clad in silk kimono, and nothing else. With his hand over his forehead, in effort to be as dramatic as possible, he breathlessly pronounced, "Oh Victoria, it is a day of the robe!" And so, it stuck. It is my go-to line whenever I have a day when getting dressed is just too much.

Be Your Own Definition

(Christine Parsons Photo)

BELIEVE THAT YOU were created with a purpose. Though there will always be naysayers, you can hear them without listening. Gather your posse and circle the wagons.

Are You Here for Good?

(Ariella Neville Photo)

Our son participated in some of the photos for artistic representation. There has been no estrangement with him.

A PERCEIVED RECONCILIATION with an estranged adult child can be a slippery slope. We are so desperate to believe that we can just begin anew, we bargain to leave a painful past behind. But the past keeps showing up. It becomes the foundation of how we interact. Blindly, with a trembling fear, we cling with both hands...sometimes, to our own detriment.

If the adult child returns as the person who left, they are still the same. All the reasons for acting out the deafening silence still exist. Their body is showing up, but with one foot out the door. We become desperate to be on our best behavior because the threat persists: "One wrong move, and I'm gone again." And so, we walk on eggshells, holding our breath with a hypersensitivity of every move we make.

We know the dire consequence of the Estrangement Elephant making its destructive stampede toward the door. Our home and loving space gets blown apart. That little twitch, making that face, or a wrong rolling of the eyes, so easily becomes the reason for a mass exodus.

The hope is that all of us will show up with accountability, understanding that one person can't fail a relationship. We can't be better together unless we are together. This requires negotiation and compromise by putting aside the blame, to leave room for improvement.

Estrangement is quite terrifying. We have no idea if or when it will find its voice. As long as silence is a threat, the rules of engagement will repeat. Behave yourself, or else. We can fix our own character defects, but we cannot fix our children.

I am careful not to wish for a past that kept me bound in judgement. I realize, now, that our togetherness was not that great. There was always an undercurrent of old pain and discomfort. Little bread crumbs that indicated where we were headed. But we chose to ignore that undercurrent by keeping it stored away. We might have thought we were moving forward, but we were stuck in the exact same place. The past continued to rule our fear-based decisions.

Our discomfort needs a conversation that will lead us to be comforted. I have lived the reality of repeated estrangement. I know the feeling of being set up to fail in spite of my effort to succeed. I tried to show up at my best. But this was to no avail. I was seen for my worst. I have asked the question, "Are you here for good?" And the answer has been, "No."

True and trustworthy reconciliation happens with truth and trust. A mutual effort to acquire new skills. Creating a mindset that will conquer future conflict. Collecting the necessary tools to build a sound foundation that everyone can rely on. Knowing that together we will celebrate our victories and share in defeat.

Have faith that broken ends can mend.

Be the Light

(Christine Parsons Photo)

THE POWER TO heal is within all of us. Reconciling the past is a decision. There is no one person who can provide light when the choice is to live in darkness. Living in the light is the gift we give ourselves.

I have been heard to say my parents are dead, but I still wish they'd change. Though I wanted my memories to provide me with a more peaceful outcome, my childhood remains intact. A journey of disappointment. Didn't I deserve better?

I am stuck with the truth. My parents did the best they could. It is not for me to say their best wasn't good enough. My judgment of their skills can't rewrite my story. So, I made it my mission to be the parent I wish I had.

I think each generation wants to create a better life for the generation that comes next. But change isn't always seen as good or correct. Perception, through the eyes of many, may find criticism and doubt. Nevertheless, we use our traumatic experiences in pursuit of being good parents. And somewhere down the line, we might be told that doing things differently has continued the cycle of disappointment.

My childhood created a rage that took hold of me as a teenager. I charged head first, plummeting on a spiral of self-destruction. My relentless focus was on blame. My inner turmoil brought me to the precipice of doom. I felt invisible. All of my destructive behavior made everything so much worse. My pain would never evolve into the change I wished to see. My parents remained unavailable, and sometimes they expressed that they wanted me gone.

Somehow, I was given the grace to realize I had a choice. It was a clear alternative: to survive and rise with self-love, or give in to the bitterness of my anger and accept that this life was void of purpose.

I chose self-love, and began the process of letting go of my past. It was a crucial decision that created a daily mindful practice to release all the things that no longer serve me. This practice is ongoing.

Shame and blame are not productive. They will

never become anything else. The moment you decide to be a warrior and eliminate your demons, you become the light, and accept what is. To all my fellow warriors: Be brave.

Solutions?

(Ariella Neville Photo)

Everything I say has answers
that rapid fire.
When I ask for solutions
you just keep telling me it is dire.

"Your failures are too many
and successes are too few."
Yet, I was once your mother
and someone that you knew.

My heart is weary and it's
difficult to give up.
But, the silence of alternatives
tells me I must stop.

Self-care requires me to
celebrate this life I have been given.
I wish you were a part of it
and estrangement wasn't driven.

I hope that you find peace
in what you must decide.
Kiss your babes for GG.
Her only choice was to abide.

I walk away knowing that
I did the best I could.
Your truth is very powerful
and I wish I understood.

Free Will

(Ariella Neville Photo)

WHEN I GAVE birth, I knew I wanted to raise my children to be strong and forthright. My hope, as they grew, was that they would develop the ability to think for themselves and be independent. So here I am, estranged from my strong and forthright daughters.

I became the mother I wish I had. My childhood was terrifying, and so I created a home that was the soft place to fall. I believed that my family would feel safe and run toward me. So here I am... watching them run away.

I spent the first year of estrangement ruminating

over every time I showed frustration, anger, and exhaustion. As it turns out, motherhood is extremely complicated. I began to believe the accusations of abuse and succumbed to their conviction. The implication evolved into a reality that they would have been better off if raised by the father.

I had no idea there was such a thing called parental alienation. I became a quick study and found a pervasive need to understand the mind of the estranged adult child. I call this my weird area of expertise. It is a knowledge that I never wanted to have.

As it turns out, the abandonment of the father was a void I could never fill. I believed I could love my children through it. Even though he kept on by suggesting: "I would have been a great dad, if your mom hadn't thrown me out." How could I have known that this seed would be planted and blossom years later? In order for him to succeed, I had to fail. One parent all good, and the other all bad. There was no room for balance or any sense of dual loyalty.

I am left in a wake of sorrow. I have read every conceivable piece of literature that might lead to a cure. I can't grasp the perception that all my motherly intentions were seen as riddled with abuse. And then I read an article by Dr Sharie Stines. "It is much easier to reject the person you know will never leave...than it is to reject the person you can barely hold onto."

Reconciliation may come. I am ready with open arms, while I hold steadfast to my truth: Emotional pain is not inflicted. Healing begins from within. Anger becomes a choice. And this is where I cannot impose my will.

Free will has a mind of its own.

Morning Means Mourning

(Ariella Neville Photo)

MORNING BREAKS. SUNLIGHT slowly creeps in, and eyes blink to accept the new day. Hopeful at first.

There is a sense of peaceful calm in those early moments. Perhaps the reverie from a dark night provided a dream filled with laughter. Children playing in the background, while you prepared afternoon snacks. Maybe attending a sporting event, where you cheered too loud for your babe. Looking in the rearview mirror with a loving gaze at the tiny head, slumped off to one side, sound asleep.

The coffee maker grinds in the distance. More blinking. Holding steadfast to that dream of a time gone by. Feet swing out of bed to touch the floor. Reality. It comes with every sunrise. The peaceful calm transforms as the truth trickles in, and recalibrates the weight of all that has been said and done. Morning means mourning.

Through every bit of sadness, hope remains. Thoughts of a productive dialogue reel inside the mind. Is today the day? Will the silence be broken? My arms are still long enough to cradle my adult child. Just give me the chance to be me.

It takes so much effort to work around the accusations that were spoken with such resentment. The heart can barely stand the pain. The mind goes into overdrive on its mission to calm the nervous system. "I love. I nurture. I feel. I think. I try. I fail. I proceed. I overcome. I persevere. I am."

I am. Does this need an explanation? What is it about me that requires a defense? Yesterday provided twenty-four hours of necessary time. Lessons of life that allow a continuation of greater intelligence. Still sitting at the edge of the bed, standing to take steps that move toward the kitchen for that morning cup of coffee. Morning means mourning.

The mind whirls. The estrangement sits front row and center. Strength is in terms of the ability to accept. Move a muscle. Change a thought. I didn't cause this. I don't control it. I can't cure it.

Thoughts wander to the grandchildren. Dance, sing, and be silly. You are part of me and therefore strong, proud, and bright. Life will always come down to the ability to laugh...even when things are not so funny.

Mourning means morning. And now it's time for lunch.

Be Part of Your Own Story

(Christine Parsons Photo)

AT THE ONSET of estrangement, I fell to earth. My heart hurt so deeply; I could not bear the pain. I would cry out, "How do I survive this?" And a voice kept repeating, "You will."

Each sunrise was filled with the intention to keep living. But the effort felt exhausting. One foot in front of the other. Feet were like blocks of cement. Every meal was dreaded. Deep breaths between bites as to not lose what I had consumed. Fear of nightfall. Sleep evaded me. Dozing off meant reliving the nightmare: my children just out of reach, my grands unaware of our DNA connection. "Who is that?" And though I would cry out, "I am your GG," my screams were mute.

The next day would come, and I would do it all over again. At night I would tuck myself in to bed and cry through my tears, "How do I survive this?" And that unmistakable voice would answer, "You will."

The hours became days. The days became months. The months became years. The choices made by others were seeping into every corner of my life. I stopped living by the suggestion that I was getting what I deserved. The implication of my unworthiness robbed me of anything good. I became a prisoner. My view of everything was disrupted by bars. "What kind of mother are you?" was the thought that reeled through my head.

"How do I survive this?" plagued my every decision. So much fear. Debilitating doubt. I was living by a definition written by others. I began to question my own motivation. Was I going to allow this to be my story? Deny myself of the many choices laid out before me? Who am I?

The answer: "I am the author." Though I still have moments of doubt and sadness, I wake each day with clarity. I can see the wealth of abundance by focusing on tiny miracles. I understand that waiting for moments of grandeur will come few and far between. I climb to greater heights and greet this life with all its imperfections. Though there is a gap of uncertainty, I

BE PART OF YOUR OWN STORY

am able to see the void as a pursuit of possibilities.

I was out on the lake in my kayak, and given a gift of alignment. A mother loon and her baby floated nearby. There was a time when I might not have appreciated the magnitude of this moment. I would have been destination-bound in a blinding effort to reach the other side of the lake. So driven as to not be on the inside of my own journey. I stopped and listened to the magic of mamma loon's voice as it echoed across the water. We floated there together for a bit, and the rest of the world melted away. My heart became warm as I realized, I had stepped in and become part of my own story. When we understand the power of simplicity, tiny miracles surround us. Peace to your mind and heart.

Never Beg for Crumbs

(Christine Parsons Photo)

THE FIRST TIME I experienced estrangement from my own child was back in 2004. I was unaware that my commitment to my children could be thwarted by an invisible coercion. I could feel the instability of suspicion growing toward me. But how could I have prepared myself for mutiny?

I had asked the father, "Can you help us with car insurance?" There were four cars registered in my name. The expenses of raising three children to adulthood was a constant juggle. Though two of them were out of the house seeking independence, the finances of parenting are ongoing. The father agreed to lend support. And that was the last thing I heard. I sent messages that went without response. I could already feel the coercion in the mystery he was creating around the assistance with car insurance.

Spring break from college found my daughter home for two weeks. The invitation for dinner at the father's was not unusual. But the whole car insurance thing was still looming. The whole situation gave me a horrible sense of foreboding. He has a talent for quietly implicating me in wrongdoing.

I imagine that this dinner was laced with innuendo. My subsequent thoughts lead me to believe the check was used as leverage. An implicated message that suggested his monetary contributions were always over and above.

I heard my daughter's car pull into the driveway. She entered through our sliding glass door into our son's room. It was very unusual for her to come home and not use the front door. My husband and I immediately looked at each other in confusion. My stomach began to churn. I knew something horrible was about to happen. When she finally entered the main part of the house, I could sense her anger. A powder keg that just needed one tiny spark. In my desperate attempt to avert the pending disaster, I asked, "How was dinner at your dad's?" That's all it took.

She flew at me, and came within inches from my face. "You can stop lying to me!! My dad is a great guy, and now I know he has been paying for everything all along." All the previous years and the constant under-tow culminated a rage I could not rein in. I hadn't felt that out of control since I was a teenager. She flicked the check for car insurance in my face. The last straw. One too many implications that the father was the hero, and my efforts as a parent, significantly sub-par.

Now don't get me wrong. We did not discuss finances with our children. In a time gone by, I had asked the father for a small increase in support. The girls were teenagers and they needed bigger things… like cars. In his words, "I am not paying you alimony." War ensued. Lawyers were hired. And every bit of ugly hit the walls. All over $20. It impacted our household with such mental upheaval, I believe we are still suffering the consequences to this day.

The demand that I stop lying about the father was a force of reckoning. A strange adrenaline hit me, and I had her up against the wall. All the years of telling me that I was never there for her. The shattering claim that everything she was and yet to become, she owed to her dad. It all ruptured in a blinding anger. "Get the F**K out of my house or I will kill you with my bare hands." Once the words were spoken, I could not take them back. Not my finest hour.

She ran into the night, and I remember the overwhelming rush of staggering defeat. My heart was so broken I couldn't eat or sleep. Within a couple of days, I called the father and asked if our daughter could live with him that summer following her freshman year in college. It was my own version of insanity in consideration of the ten years of his counter-parenting.

There were no brakes on this runaway train. The seeds had been planted with the intention of gross manipulation. And now, they were harvesting in spades. She truly believed that I didn't love her, which has become an ongoing mindset. The first estrangement began, and it went on for six years.

I remember hearing that my daughter was taking a semester abroad during her sophomore year in college. I hated getting these nuggets of information, as they never came from her. She would sporadically reply to an e-mail, or sometimes we would talk on the phone. It was January and the information about her semester abroad was thrown at me in the supermarket. My baby girl was leaving for South America for five months. She would board a plane within the coming week.

I sucked up my pride and called the father's house. When she knew it was me, her voice became monotone. Even though I had barely seen her in over a year, I tried to be chirpy. I called because I needed to hear it from her, "Where will you be going?" I asked so simply. Her response assaulted me. "Anything you want to know about me, you can ask Alice (the stepmom)."

My reaction was immediate. I began screaming and sobbing incoherently. Defending my honor. Begging for a mother's right to know her own child. She began to laugh, and interrupted my tirade of grief, "Listen to yourself. You sound ridiculous." And she hung up on me. Later it would be told that my screaming was at her and not for her. It became, yet, one more case of my gross mental instability and propensity to be abusive.

I am estranged from her today for the third time. Both daughters have agreed in their effort against me. They present themselves as a united front. The years of silence have produced five grandchildren with whom I have no contact. It has been strongly suggested that I am getting what I deserve. "This is not fixable." Even though there has been no attempt to repair what is broken. "We will never forgive you." The conclusion without a discussion.

I do recall what I said before I went into that blinding hysteria prior to my daughter's semester abroad. The horrible suggestion that I call the stepmother for information found a moment of clarity, "I am your mother. I will not beg for crumbs." I think of this every time I feel the propensity to plead for mercy. To cry, "UNCLE!" and beg for all the things that are lost.

I remind myself that I am a good, kind, and loving mother, grandmother, wife, and friend. I am human, and so beautifully flawed.

How Is Today?

(Christine Parsons Photo)

I AM LEARNING that most people say what makes them feel better. Adult child estrangement and grandparent alienation is an extremely uncomfortable topic. The general public will squirm, at the mere mention. A quick solution is offered to make the conversation come to an abrupt end. Almost a pleading, "Do we have to talk about this?" You can see it in their faces.

Quickly comes the suggestion that you might move on. Or perhaps commit to the action of letting go by simply releasing your grip on worry or doubt. Just make a decision to wash all your cares away like a sand-castle at high tide. But these are complicated matters. And solutions sound hollow.

I had breakfast, the other day, with a dear friend who lost her twenty-two-year-old daughter to complications of diabetes. It is a most grievous loss. If you have followed my writing, you have read my urge to give pain a purpose. My friend created a foundation to honor her daughter with all proceeds to benefit those suffering from Type 1. A broken heart that evolved through the opportunity to create light through circumstances of darkness. By helping others, she is able to gain a sense of direction.

My friend has said to me so many times, "I know I will see my girl again. She is always with me. And I know if she were here, she would be right here. But you live each day knowing your daughters are out there somewhere. This has to be so much harder."

When we grieve for those who are still alive, there is a strange sense of wonder and confusion. Will this ever end? Can we reconcile? It presents us with a reality of gaining information when we would rather remain ignorant. Unsolicited news always pushes a mental feeling of physically doubling over. It is an effort of the heart to remain standing.

My friend understands the ongoing process of grief. She shared something that resonated with me so deeply. It has been twelve years since she lost her daughter (2010). And over time, she has developed a handful of dear souls who empathize with her daily struggle. Never an implication that it is possible to get over it. We get over a cold. Instead of asking, "How are you," they will ask, "How is today?" Something so simple that frees her to speak her truth whether it's a good day or bad.

I understand this journey of estrangement is difficult and beyond words. I admit to the challenge of listening to people prattle on about their children and grandchildren. But when I am in the presence of those who will stop for a brief moment to acknowledge my heart, as if to say, "How is today?" I am able to feel their joy.

When our feelings are validated, we know we are being heard.

DNA

(Ariella Neville Photo)

I WAS AT the dump yesterday. My mission was to get in and out as quickly as possible. A woman I hadn't seen in years was running toward me across the parking lot. She was extremely excited to share that she and her daughter follow my daughter's blog. "OMG... all the traveling she does with her children!!"

I stood dumbfounded. All my effort to block social media does not ensure that bystanders won't verbally accost me with an unsolicited visual. Immediately, I made it very clear that there was a gross lack of a relationship. I used my words very carefully in order to turn conversation to a different topic. "I have not spoken to either of my daughters in over six years." To my horror, she was adamant that I should hear her voice: "But the way she brings her children to other countries." My head was imploding as my internal dialogue reeled, "Please stop talking!!"

Out loud, I kept reiterating the lack of relationship. She refused my effort to shut it down. Instead, it was as if she held a hot poker, jabbing me with questions and information. I felt like I was a witness to a crime. She was like an attorney sent in, for the sole purpose, of getting me to confess the truth. I just kept stuttering, "I have no idea what she does with her kids. I have never met them." And she continued her demand for a connection. I am the mother, after all.

My stomach was flip-flopping. My nervous system was on high alert. This was a strange and wicked suggestion that, though I haven't spoken to my daughter in years, I must follow her doings and whereabouts. DNA would certainly provoke me to align with her journey on social media whether we have a relationship or no relationship at all. Acquiring a false sense of order to bragging rights about her and her children. A bizarre level of ownership to exude motherly pride.

I stood face to face with this woman as my breath became an effort. Even though I grew a human inside my womb, raised her from infancy to adulthood, and know she walks this earth with my biology, our DNA is not an emotional connection.

That feeling of family being everything is realized when you are everything to family. There is no telepathy brought on by a once, existing umbilical cord. Estrangement cuts the bonds of compromise and negotiation These are the crucial components to a healthy relationship. As long as silence is used as a weapon, it guarantees the propensity to keep yesterday in the present.

There comes a point where there is no option to pretend that bad things never happened. Unearthing painful chapters is difficult and it is work. It takes courage to face our demons. For now, my girls are not ready. I have gained a sense of compassion around this. Giving myself the beauty of abundance as my life is not based on this one thing. "There are only two ways to live your life. One is as though nothing is a miracle. The other is as if everything is." ~ Albert Einstein~

Can Your Adult Child Forget You?

(Ariella Neville Photo)

WHEN I AM out of step with people I love, it becomes all-consuming. My brain is in search of solutions. My heart needs to speak a dialogue that will heal.

The arguing feels like pushing rope uphill. It can't move forward. We defend ourselves from a place of guilt, because we know we lost our temper...more than once. Parenting is complicated and at times messy. There have been moments of anger, tears, and butting heads with significant force. Could we have done better? Perhaps, if there were goggles that gave us the wisdom of hindsight. Otherwise, impossible to gain the knowledge needed for tomorrow. The lessons are happening today.

People are always doing the best they can with what they know. My friend has a wonderful quote, "Hard tellin', not knowin." I don't believe that any parent wakes in the morning with the intention of creating Adult Child Estrangement. We bumble and fall along this road called parenthood. Mistakes were made, but should never be seen as failure. Our experiences become lessons to proceed with greater intelligence. The punishment of estrangement is a cruel solution. No one can mend a broken relationship by themselves.

So, that feeling of panic, out of sight out of mind. The desperation of sending a text, e-mail, voice mail, as a reminder of who you are and how you love. Every time you think that your memory has become selective amnesia, ask yourself, "Could I forget I have an estranged child?"

Each one of us has something in our past that we wish was different. We all have painful memories that beg to be erased, and yet it remains. There are no do-overs. It is with precision that our mind eventually tells our heart, "My emotional pain is not inflicted. It has become a choice."

Painful experiences don't wash away. These chapters are written in concrete. The only way to come to terms with the past is to forgive. This is a verb, and it requires forward thinking. To sit in resentment is the pill we swallow waiting for others to fall. When we free ourselves of anger, we are able to make peaceful decisions. Choices born of chaos create more chaos.

    I continue to pray for all of our estranged children to shine light in dark places. Trust that you have not been forgotten.

Fragmentation

(Ariella Neville Photo)

ESTRANGEMENT. IN THE beginning, it seemed I was the sole target. I was getting what I deserve. And I took it all on my shoulders. The incessant apologies didn't stop with my pleading. Not just for me, but for all who remain innocent. Dear souls who stand at the periphery, yet silenced by collateral damage.

The word of the estrangement spread. Like spilled milk, the circumstances washed over my entire community. They joined hands to grieve with me for all that is lost.

Years passed, with a silence so deafening that prayers

began with hope of a whisper. But nothing was heard except the sound of wind against the house.

I am better when I am peaceful. As much as it hurts, it is worth the effort to move away from anger. My attempts at contact have evolved me to a place of no expectation. If the extension of the olive branch is not reciprocated, I am alright. My own heart is served so that I may be at peace with my choices.

When issues go unresolved, they sit on your chest like a giant boulder. If given the chance to break the silence, you might begin with small talk. But eventually that mass of granite makes it hard to breathe, because the issues still sit on your chest.

Our circumstances find my family as a whole divided in two. My husband, son, and I are the amputated branch of our family tree. Though we are very much alive, we are not seen. This makes it necessary to blur the truth. Stories have to be told. Reconciliation has become very complicated. There are too many people that have become involved. All the adult issues have spread to the innocent who have no voice. The spilled milk has seeped into every crack and crevice.

I do work hard not to assign blame. Even when the father condescends, "I don't blame our daughters for not wanting you around their children. Nobody ever knows when you are going to snap!!" It is most difficult to come to terms with this horrible accusation that I would actually harm my grandchildren. I console my heart. There is no control over what people say about me. My posse doesn't need to be convinced.

Sometimes my son will share his feelings of abandonment: "I had two sisters who I loved and looked up to. And now, I don't." A split-second solution has resulted in long-term consequences. The eerie stillness pushes away the work that needs to be done.

There is much internal conflict. It requires the peeling of an onion, layer by layer. One issue at a time. Uncomfortable conversations. An emotional marathon. The ability to show up. Be accountable. Asking of one another, "What role did I play in the things that went wrong?"

Our son approached me six years into the silence. He was ready to reach out to his sisters. "I am free of anger and expectation." He shared. I didn't want to be a Debbie Downer, but felt I needed to advise, "The estrangement is not just between me and the girls anymore. Healing with your siblings has become collective work with all three of you. This will require some difficult conversations. Otherwise, small talk will remain small talk, and the issues will sit on your chest like a mass of granite.

He called to tell me there was a lunch date on the calendar. The meeting with his older sister ended with a stomachache. His nervous system raced into high gear. The discussion of movies, books and the weather kept the conversation moving, but not forward. The boulder sat in the middle of the table waiting to demonstrate its massive weight. Anytime the discussion began to skirt hot topics, fear pulled it in another direction. Nothing got solved, and they haven't spoken since. My family is not ready to heal.

In as much as we would like to wipe the slate clean, it won't erase trauma. No matter how tenderly we walk on eggshells, they crack beneath our feet. The foundation is too fragile, and not a safe place to build. There is something to be said for the expression: "The truth will set you free."

I try to imagine a hero from the other side of my divided family. Someone who has the strength and the courage to move the granite mass from our chest. At long last, we will breathe freely in a common pursuit to be one family.

Fragmentation blows families apart. It guarantees that we will talk about each other, but not to each other. From our separate corners, we create stories that are full of mistruths. We are like a puzzle that requires careful consideration. Searching for the place where each piece will fit. Mindful that we will not look the same as before. Hoping for better. Having faith that these broken ends can mend.

Answers?

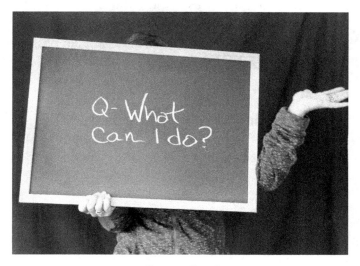

(Ariella Neville Photo)

"WHAT CAN I do to fix this?" We have wracked our brains over a gesture or a string of words that would bridge the gap. We need to believe, if given the chance, we could cradle the bruised emotions, and envelope our child with love and warmth. Blame has planted the seed that this is ours to fix. What lies ahead, however, is a mountain of emotional work. Even if we get in shape enough to reach the summit alone, the effort remains singular. Those who are not able or willing can't fully understand this experience in words.

When dealing with a loved one who remains in a place of anger, it is difficult to create a language of peace. The bitterness rises to the surface like cream on top of milk. It rules the dialogue. Though you might try to inject compassion, it is more often than not, returned with chaos.

Our instinct is to nurture. But our love is denied. Unwittingly, we were sent on a path unchosen through circumstances that we would never sign up for. It is crucial, at this point, to take back your power. Self-care requires us to stay inside our own head. To remain on our front porch, without worry of what is happening next door.

It is perfectly natural, this wanting to take on our children's discomfort and make it our own. We, desperately, grasp at anything that might make it stop. It feels like a blinding search for solutions. Though the path to healing might look crystal clear to you, it is not so for the estranged child.

The family as a whole must arrive at a place of agreement. Meeting face to face, and leaving high emotion at the door. Knee-jerk reactions will only result in more kicking. By replacing fear with love, we are able to calmly share our discomforts. Together we can recognize the simplicity of releasing the grip on anger by making peaceful decisions. Otherwise, our choices are void of logic, and the cycle will repeat.

I have learned the value of hitting the pause button. There was a time when I was a valiant right fighter.

Time has given me the opportunity to understand that speaking from a place of calm keeps you mindful of the issue. Screaming pain will keep you emotional. When our mind is at peace, so is our dialogue.

My hope for all of our adult children is the realization that this can get better. The uncomfortable conversations of reconciliation can lead us to mindful discussions, by speaking the truth that will move us forward. We need only look in the rear-view mirror to see how far we have come. When the question rises, "What can I do?" Commit to self-care, because if you don't put the oxygen mask on you first, you won't be able to assist anyone else. Peace to your tender hearts.

You

(Ariella Neville Photo)

FINGER-POINTING IS AN exhausting pursuit. In the throes of anger, the word "you" has the tendency to become abusive. I think of how I feel when I'm on the receiving end of blame. My mind goes quickly to everything I can say to hit below the belt. I need the other person to hurt as much as I do.

On the flip side, I shut down when someone is screaming at me in a horrible tone of blame. Their voice becomes Charlie Brown's teacher: "Whah whah whah whah whah." The result turns my effort to speak with intention, always mindful of the desired result.

What is the end game?

I was recently disappointed and subsequently furious with a friend. I had the date and time on the calendar, but she didn't show up. I texted, "Where are you?" and waited for a response. Every minute that passed only proved to increase my anger.

That feeling of abandonment hit hard. I was stuck with the impression that I am insignificant. So small, that I don't matter. But I had to think about the overall nature of our relationship. Would she hurt me intentionally? The answer was no. This was a huge "ah-ha" moment. Most of us don't hurt other people with intention.

When she received my attempt at contact, she responded by telling me that she had just returned home. She was out with another friend and no longer had time to get together. It felt so flippant and without care. I was seething. And because my nervous system was blowing up, I hit pause. My emotions of retaliation needed to simmer.

The next day I reached out from a place of calm, sticking to the issue that caused the feelings. Why was I hurt? Because I felt that she blew me off without a thought or a care. To the contrary, she sent an immediate response with a sincere apology. Though I had the date firmly planted, she believed our wires got crossed. If I was inclined to right fight, I would have accused her with my pointed finger and claim that she messed up. But this was not going to lead us down a better path.

Her apology offered me a validation of my feelings, but I still needed to heal. The pain of abandonment was not going to magically disappear. I had work to do. Her ability to say, "I'm sorry" was certainly part of the process. But the art of letting go of my hurt feelings required a commitment. The bottom line and the healthy alternative: I did not want to hold on to my anger.

Yes, I could have told her she sucks as a friend. But that would be something to say if I no longer cared about the relationship. My mindset was to make it better, not worse. The end game always in focus. Therefore, our interaction to resolve led us to higher ground. The friendship has been preserved, and my hurt from the experience slowly dissolved. This is the power of productive dialogue.

Being an estranged parent seemingly renders us powerless. We stand accused of causing harm with intention. But this is perception and not truth. Our direction is not determined by another person, nor is our self-worth. Never let another person define who you are or tell you which way to go.

It is difficult, at best, to dismiss the thoughts of wishing your adult children could see you for who you are by revisiting the days when you were everything to your family. It is this tendency to ruminate over every moment that wasn't so pretty that locks us in to our past. The truth is, we have all done and said things we wish to take back. Being human isn't perfect.

In these moments of doubt, stick to what you know. Finger-pointing only creates more finger-pointing. Screaming emotions will never offer peaceful solutions. When we choose to engage, it is a decision to arrive with integrity. No matter what bait is being thrown, we don't need to show up for every fight. And yes, there are times when our temper gets the best of us. It feels like eating a big slice of chocolate cake when you are trying so hard to make healthy choices. Once consumed, you feel mad that you gave into temptation. But this doesn't mean you've lost the battle. The diet of wellbeing can continue tomorrow. It is the opportunity to begin anew with better self-control. Practice calm reactions. You got this. Be kind to yourself. You have right now.

What We Believe as True

(Ariella Neville Photo)

IT TAKES A long time to formulate a belief. When faced with opposition, we push back at anyone or anything that threatens what we believe to be true. Great time and effort have been put into the structure that represents a safe haven. We are all comfortable when we see something we know we can trust. Any attempt to dismantle this truth is seen as a threat.

Estranged parents just want to be heard. They pose an opposition to the belief that they never showed up when needed most. A desperate plea to be given one moment to profess their unconditional love that will

WHAT WE BELIEVE AS TRUE

lead to forgiveness. Begging for the opportunity to replace the chaos with peace.

If only we could come together as a family in a discussion of the truth, keeping the focus on blending our beliefs to find common ground. Together, we might find a place where we can meet in the middle for all future interaction.

It is our deepest desire to move our children into this space. But they have to want to be moved. They must be willing to risk the deconstruction of what they have worked so hard to build. This requires a huge change in direction. They have grown comfortable in the silence because it blocks out controversy. To part with their safe haven is a giant leap into uncertainty.

I pray for the day of agreement. Holding steadfast to the belief that the salvation of our family relationships is worth the effort. Entering each interaction with an open mind. Allowing the process to unfold. At long last, creating change for the better.

Planning

(Christine Parsons Photo)

HOW DO YOU plan to be estranged from your own child? When I think about it, I am in a place of wonder. The universe did not listen to me. I, vehemently, told it this was not the way life was supposed to be.

I realize my fragility of power and any notion of control. I am so sad that I can't impose my will. My family has become afraid of painful emotions, and I just want to cure it.

When we devise concrete plans, we are often disappointed. It only takes one person, place, or thing to blur what we thought we would see. "We make plans and the Goddess laughs!" said my friend after breaking her leg from a slow fall off her bike. Yes, I concurred, "It takes a lot for the universe to synchronize all the moving parts to align with the vision of our expectations!!"

My son shared this quote from The Dark Tower by Stephen King:

"Ka (fate) like the wind it blows, and all of your best laid plans stand before it like a barn in a fierce storm."

This is life.

Gaslighting

(Ariella Neville Photo)

IN 2016, I grabbed ahold of any literature that would help me make sense of my mystifying reality. Everything I said was nonsensical. On my search of discovery, I did find articles that helped to take the edge off my pain. My heightened awareness gave me the ability to name the beast, but I could not change its spots. The challenges of communication remain.

My human interaction, as an estranged parent, finds me hypervigilant. Sadly, my expectations of most people are quite low. Once your own child wants nothing to do with you, everybody else is suspect. I am constantly discerning, "Are you greeting me with sincerity?" Or, "Are you spending time with me in order to unearth my defects?" Or, "Do you just need to make S**T up?"

There are some relationships that I have grown to trust. Those friendships that span decades are made up of many shared moments. This is where I have been duped into seeing people for who I want them to be. Sometimes a sad truth will hit me like a two-by- four. I call it selective deafness, because I block out the dialogue that yells loud and clear, "When you need me most, I won't show up for you." And worse, they become an adversary on my quest to stay sane. Living within my reality has its challenges.

It makes sense to seek out those who are emotionally intelligent. Gather your posse and circle the wagons. Be with the people who will never gloss over the years of estrangement, and how they've become part of you. Give yourself the grace of being seen without an expectation that you should be different. It is a process to greet each day one by one. This path unchosen teaches us that acceptance is not a permanent address. It is OK to cycle up, down, and around all the five stages of grief: denial, anger, bargaining, depression, and acceptance.

This journey has taught me to compartmentalize my friendships. My fair-weather friends are not the people I call in a storm. I engage with them when the sun is shining. And then there are those friends who will show up in the middle of a tornado. You know they will be at your door in minutes of your cry for help. Sometimes we believe that the decades spent with another person offers us a guaranteed amount of empathy. But solid relationships are not born of time, they are born of reciprocating emotions. New friendships can enter our lives in the beat of a heart. But that doesn't mean they are with us forever.

The experience of selective deafness takes away the right to be surprised. When someone keeps telling you who they are, it is up to us to listen. It's a difficult task when you have designed someone in the image of who you want them to be. And so, enters sadness and disappointment.

My study of human behavior keeps telling me that friendship has nothing to do with the calendar. It is the quality of time, not the quantity. I have grown a keen sense of truth around this. Yes, I have reorganized my address book. It doesn't mean I have to call it quits. I just look at the weather before I pick up the phone.

As my journey unfolds, I proceed with greater intelligence, and gratitude for the opportunity in gains toward my personal growth. Peace to those who walk this path.

A Wedding

(Christine Family Album)

IN SEPTEMBER OF 2010, I moved into another chapter. I was Mother of the Bride, and became a

Mother-in-Law. My heart was full that day, as I felt an expansion. Different families would now be one. The bride and groom supported by their community as a whole. It was with eager anticipation that I looked forward to what was yet to come.

I was about to walk down the aisle in procession to my assigned seat. It was a moment of commemoration, thinking back on all the years I actively parented my eldest child. I felt an overwhelming sense of unity. Our blended family was finally able to come together in peace. It was a split-second decision, when I wrapped my arm through the arm of the stepmother. It was a feeling that we should walk down the aisle together. So many sudden emotions wafted over me. No matter the challenges of raising children in two different households, it took each one of us to get here. There was an overwhelming feeling of pride as we hailed the crowd and celebrated our adult children. A glorious chapter written in one day.

As I have often said, it takes a lot of moving parts to synchronize with the vision of our expectations. We adopt a belief and count on it as we interact in this great wide world. If our beliefs are threatened, it requires a lot of force to rewrite what we thought was true. It never would have occurred to me that all our moving parts would run in separate directions.

So much has changed since that day. Beliefs have been redirected. And I have been written out of their story. Today (September 10th) is the anniversary of my daughter's wedding. I pause for a moment to acknowledge my feelings. This has become an important part of my process. My nervous system already calculates the day on the calendar. It's OK to be sad.

Sometimes we just need a Day of the Robe, but never making it a comfortable place to live. The next sunrise is in motivation to move a muscle and change a thought. Gather your posse and circle the wagons. Peace.

The Cause-the Cure-the Control

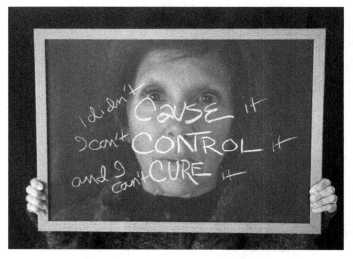

(Ariella Neville Photo)

MY HEART TELLS my head, "You are such a failure. Your most important job...and you suck at it." Since 2016, though not as frequent, this reel still plays in my head.

Reaching out to other estranged parents has helped me to find common ground. Through the same challenging experience, I found the people who talk the same language. Sadly, it is the all the other broken-hearted parents who understand that this is not a simple argument. Our children won't just, "Get over it." And somehow, we learn that this is not our fault.

Accused as being socially inept, mean-spirited, self-absorbed, or abusive. From the ashes we rise with the grace to continue our loving intention. Believe that you are here with a purpose.

I am strong for most days, and proceed with kindness. Today, however, is a day of that self-deprecating internal dialogue. I am so emotionally paralyzed; I can't even take my own advice. The sad part of this journey is there are good days and bad. Being human comes with doubt and a variety of other things. I'm tired and I feel weak. The effort to ask light to enter my darkness is too heavy.

I am so sad right now. I must sit quietly and process in effort to meet the appointments on my calendar. Nestled in my pajamas and morning coffee, I wish today could be a Day of the Robe. In an hour, I have to get in my car.

Adult Child Estrangement and Grandparent Alienation are powerful forces. With one hand tied behind their back, they have the strength to knock me on my ass. Though I try to get up, the reality flattens me.

I move around a bit. Commence with bilateral stimulation. Anything that requires left-right action. Emotional right brain meets the logic of the left brain and a marriage of mindful decisions unfolds. I will be OK. I acknowledge my sadness. It is valid.

I have said many times, "It is OK to be sad. But it is never OK to be incapacitated." My scheduled appointments will pull me away from my gloom. This estrangement was never my choice. I desperately wanted the uncomfortable conversations. I was ready to name the issues and the past traumas. That unspoken dialogue plagues me as the boxes of unresolved conflict remain unchecked.

But when pain and anger rule our thoughts, our decisions are based on the discomfort. This is not productive, and most often to the contrary. We are best to search solutions when we feel at peace. This keeps us in check, when we feel the temptation to hit below the belt. I admit to the many times I wanted to write hateful letters. Hurt gets confused with anger. I am learning to laugh even when things aren't so funny. Smiling helps me to remain kind, even in the face of adversity.

There is no doubt that I am bamboozled by this estrangement. It has taken time in realizing that I did not cause it. No matter what went wrong, silence guarantees that I can't cure it. And the biggest lesson of all: I can't control it. Any sense of order can go no further than the end of our nose.

The shame and blame can bring us to our knees. All the horrible accusations of owning the way other people feel. Human interaction comes at the risk of bringing on undesired emotions. Herein lies the choice. To process in order to release, or hold on. After

THE CAUSE-THE CURE-THE CONTROL

a while, holding on becomes a job. The continual reel of repurposing painful events is exhausting. My questions and uncertainty beg: "How long and how far do you want to carry this burden?" This is what I would ask of my daughters…if only they wanted to listen.

It's time to get in my car. I have an appointment that needs to be met. So, I turn up the radio. Distract my thoughts to move into this moment. I sing out loud to a familiar song. As I drive, I am suddenly aware of being present in right now. And this moment is perfect.

Does the Punishment Fit the Crime?

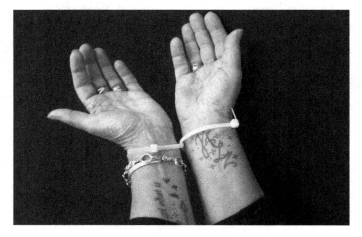

(Ariella Neville Photo)

SOMETIMES I FEEL that Adult Child Estrangement is a life sentence without chance for parole. There have been many accusations. The evidence appears circumstantial.

The charges are understood by everyone in the court-room. There is a consensus that putting me behind bars saves others. My hatred and mental instability are obvious. And so, I am found guilty, though my fight for innocence continues.

The estranged parent hangs on every spoken word. The verbs might hold the key to unlocking this view from behind bars. What was so unforgiveable that this trial without a jury finds us too far gone? And the memories flood...all those years of loving parenthood. But it's like being in a desert, and those joyful images are just a mirage. Our thirst overwhelms us, and the only water is filled with every moment we lost our temper.

I will share that my daughters had some major throes with their own temper tantrums. Yes, they were between the ages of three and six. High-pitched screaming that required me to remove them from public places. They have been carried out of supermarkets, and I have asked for to-go boxes at restaurants. All despairing when our differences hinged on sugary snacks vs. healthy choices. Now why would I shame them for something they did so long ago? They are no longer those people, and neither are we.

Every day that we live is the gain of greater life experience. We use that knowledge and base our decisions on what we know at the time. Evolution commands that we are all in constant transition of who we are yet to become. To judge someone through the eyes of hindsight is never fair. To shame someone for who they were yesterday is fruitless. The minute we act and react, it is already in the past. Let's talk about right now.

We can't tell our adult children to stop feeling the way they do. All the apologies in the world won't make them feel better. When the emotions remain, there is a persistence to hold on. Sadly, we don't have access to the release button. It is so hard for parents to see the line where our children's pain begins and where we end. This is not our work.

What a lesson in our fragility of power. The teaching of control. Despite the knowledge that there is no way to commandeer people, places, and things, I still wish for the call that will connect. I imagine myself joyfully transitioning to the dialogue meant to heal. I long for the answers to my long-standing question, "What do I need to do to move us to a better place?"

We can't be better together unless we're together. Yes, the parties involved can go off in separate corners and learn to live apart. It might appear as some semblance of forward motion, but the unresolved conflict remains. The belief that estrangement is the best choice finds a daily process of justifying the giant void in communication.

I used to believe that the past should stay in the past. But this only resulted in my walking on eggshells. The elephant was asking for its next meal, and I couldn't get it to leave. Once estrangement becomes the solution, it is the first place we go the minute uncomfortable emotions rise. It can take one simple word that ignites a reaction. But you rarely know what word will have the same results as waving a red cape at a bull.

I have tried, in earnest, during family occasions, to be on my best behavior. To exhibit myself as socially appropriate. To smile from ear to ear when those who cast suspicion, enter the room. I act adoringly to the people who stir up controversy and cast doubt. Mindfully ingratiating myself to behave and be humbled by their company. But when your people want you to fail, you will fail.

It is with piercing eyes they wait for your wrongdoing. Did you just cross your legs to the right when everyone else crosses to the left? Inevitably, you will say somebody's name in the wrong tone of voice, or perhaps have the audacity to sigh, roll your eyes, pick your nose…etc.

I wish I had the perfect lawyer who could force the hands of justice to set us all free. Alas, these circumstances are collective and require everyone to show up and work the problem. True and trustworthy reconciliation requires group accountability of "what" went wrong, not "who" went wrong. We didn't get here by ourselves.

I have released the proposal of accusations. Through the support of my community, I am able to walk my personal truth. I recommend steering clear of those who offer blanket solutions (e.g., move on, let go, get over it). Be with those who can sit with you on those sad days. Empathy allows us to see through the eyes of another, even if we don't share the same experience. A simple offering: "This must hurt so much."

Believe you are here with a purpose, and be kind in the wake of adversity.

Letter from My Daughter 2001

(Ariella Neville Photo)

Mom,

I'm sitting in my apartment right now, and feel compelled to write, and tell you how much I love and appreciate you. At a time of such great loss, I feel like I need to reach out to those that I hold dear. All through my life, you have been my rock. Without you, I don't know what would have become of me. Your love and support have gotten me through the toughest and most challenging aspects of life. These past two weeks have been a time of horrific loss. The world is struggling with the devastation following 911. I feel like the bond between us has only gotten stronger, despite the mass devastation all around us. Nothing else makes me happier. I do not take our relationship for granted. I know that I am truly blessed to have you in my corner. I only wish that when I have children, I will be as good a mother as you are. You are a true inspiration, and I love you with all my heart.

Love,
Zoey

I came across this letter while going through a pile of old papers. I have read my daughter's words over and over again. The sentiment expressed reminds me of a time gone by. I was permitted the grace to bumble in my motherhood. Forgiveness came with those tough moments when I wasn't at my best. I was allowed to fall down, and praised for the way I got up. She used to refer to me as, "Amazing."

The expression of her sentiment can't just evaporate. I believe she still feels this way deep inside her heart. I think of her as being covered by a cloak that keeps her safe. For now, the reasons for her choices are something I have to respect. They are her choices to make.

It's easy to take these circumstances personally. The truth? It's not really about us. The experience speaks to the conflict and the ability to resolve the past. When we become emotionally paralyzed, so enters the need to find fault in others.

Estranged parents hear advice to let go. This is an evolutionary process of all the things that no longer serve us. The suggestion appears like a light switch, with an on-off button. It sounds so easy. Just let go.

I have been lost in my attempt to enact this simple solution. Time helped me to realize that this takes effort. It requires me to show up every day, unencumbered by the truth. I am estranged from my own child. Most days are difficult. It's hard to be in a Zen-like state every day. Sometimes I have to really work on soft and pretty, when life feels sharp and ugly. No matter how many years go by, the tears still come.

All of these emotions are truly challenging. Our quest is to travel through despair in order to discover joy. Though they sit in opposition, they both create feelings of great intensity.

My path continues to spiral me through old stuff. It's hard not to reflect on that time gone by. But with the gain of emotional intelligence, I can use my experiences to guide me in the present. I take time to pray for my daughter's growth. Hope springs eternal. I try to imagine that someday something will click and lead her to search within. The power of healing is always there. It is a mindful approach that takes practice. A commitment to want change for the better.

Peace to your tender hearts.

How It Fades....

(Christine Parsons Family Album)

MY GRANDDAUGHTER'S BIRTHDAY was last week (September 2021). I had totally forgotten. And then I felt the onset of a sudden and sickening feeling. I realized her special day had passed without my formulating a telepathic message.

At first, I spoke a quiet whisper to acknowledge that she was now six. But then an undeniable doom washed over me when I realized she was actually seven. My emotions imploded, and I began to cry. My husband replied to my despair, "Well what are you supposed to do?" So many calendars have gone empty of invitations. My memories take me back to when this all began. I continue to rip the pages of the months and years. It is with a heartbroken recollection that I think of a time when it was important that I be there.

The last time I saw my granddaughter she asked, "Are you Mommy's friend?" My heart was not able to go into a whole rendition of how I am actually her grandmother. She knows these familial relationships. She anticipates their visits and recognizes them immediately. By now, even if she thought I was Mommy's friend...the memory of me has surely faded.

And so, my memories are fading too. I am not quite able to summon up what it would feel like to actually see my grandchildren. What would that look like? I summon up an image of my being present in milestone events. The freedom to be privy to their daily lives. Knowing all the things that are simple like: sleeping habits, what they like to eat, their favorite color, best subject at school, etc. I can hear my grandson's three-year-old voice: "GG, can I have PBJ toast?" A loving ritual with its microscopic simplicity. Comforting and familiar.

I had once felt that being a grandmother was my reward for all the hard decisions I had to make as a parent. I try not to feel as though I'm being punished, but it has been suggested I am getting what I deserve.

When I think of the ripple effect that estrangement spills onto, who is this really hurting? A friend said to me, "Trust that anyone who cares about you is so sad." A community grieves knowing the loss.

Friendships have ended as loyalty shifts. It's like a divorce, and eventually people choose sides. Grief rewrites your address book. I am so grateful to those who have no desire to fix me. And I have to keep considering that, when people dole out advice, they are often saying what makes them feel better.

Wow, I forgot my granddaughter's birthday. Is this a good thing? Perhaps I should think of it as being spared. Alleviated of the work it takes to minimize the anguish. Saving my heart, the despair of going off the rails. My imagination is crystal clear. I can see the family gatherings as if I am watching from a distance. The rhythmic dance as my DNA flourishes without me. This is where my head wants to go. I have decided that my forgetfulness is a shield of protection. It guards me from the things I cannot control. More emotional intelligence that offers strength and courage in the face of adversity. Peace of mind.

Introduction to a Private Support Group

(Jeffrey Simpson Photo)

HELLO TO ALL your tender hearts. To those who poured yourself into the love and nurture of your children. To you, who showed up every day. To each mother and father who walks this path unchosen. Though I am new to this group, I am not new to the challenges of silence. It has become my weird area of expertise that aligns me with frustration. Learning about the pain my loved ones choose to hold close to the vest. The solutions are becoming complicated. My family is like a big ball of knotted yarn. The sweater is complete, but it is badly misshapen. It's a bunch of lumps and bumps that proved too time consuming to untangle. So, we just kept knitting.

There was a time when I begged. I pleaded in urgency, "I love you. I want you in my life. What do I need to do to move us to a better place?" Silence. I fell to earth. The answers were never solutions. It was either an eerie quiet or more revelations of my character defects. They are described as so heinous that forgiveness is not an option.

I have theories to the maladies that plague my family. Divorce, counter-parenting, psychological warfare. Forced to make decisions based on the path of least resistance. I have not been forgiven, and we continue to battle. That simmering anger that becomes a silent coercion. Each day is met in the wake of collateral damage as my family has been blown to bits.

The emotional unrest creates choices based on feelings. They see me as a monster. They have painted over the image of the loving human who was always on the side-lines cheering the loudest. I begged the father to facilitate healing. I know how estrangement hurts the innocent. I have been told, "You are getting what you deserve."

My daughters' feelings of abandonment developed a hole in their hearts. I thought I could love them through it, but it was a void I could never fill. And so, the emotions grew with a need to assign blame. "It is easier to reject the person you know will never leave, than it is to reject the person you can barely hold on to." ~Dr. Sharie Stines~

I have had much time to contemplate my grief. It is a process of learning how to celebrate life in the wake of Adult Child Estrangement. I think of it as seeing the forest for the trees without focusing on that one broken limb. I have no power over how long and how far my daughters choose to carry this burden. I see it as a giant mass that could be broken up and shared. Each one of us could shoulder the piece that we need to own. And then, perhaps, we might live a life unencumbered by the past. We could finally move forward, and tell our story as a whole.

Sadly, reconciliation, for now, looks impossible. A Pandora's Box that, once opened, can never be closed. Unearthing all those past traumas that will revive the pain of the memory. But this has to be done as a means to an end. When we allow our past to become part of who we are, it creates purpose. We gain a sense of direction that offers the ability to proceed in kindness. I love this saying: Use your past. Don't be used by it.

INTRODUCTION TO A PRIVATE SUPPORT GROUP

There are certain chapters in everyone's life that won't be remembered without heartache and challenge. Trauma is never not trauma. However, taking the time to reconcile these experiences will soothe the memory. It will stop showing up every time there is emotional conflict. Those feelings will no longer determine the future.

My heart begs for my girls to end this journey filled with pain. I have hope that they will release the anger in order to free their own hearts. I pray for light to shine in dark places. Peace to all who walk this path unchosen.

Emotional Paralysis

(Christine Parsons Photo)

A FRIEND ONCE asked, "Would you kick someone in a wheelchair and demand they walk?" This said when I was full of expectation. I was in dire need of another person to show up for me, though I knew they had limited resources. We can grow with a repertoire of words, but lack of empathy has a different language. When we expect people to give us what they don't have, it creates disappointment. Our estranged loved ones don't have the words to resolve the issues. And so it goes; "The naked woman can't give you her shirt."

I am a product of estrangement, and both of my

parents took silence to the grave. My families could not manifest a productive dialogue. My formative years were spent knowing that there were very few who could operate in my best interest. As a child, I had no voice.

We get hurt and we get angry. Most often, this turns to a mindset of retaliation. We commit to right fighting, screaming while pointing fingers driven by the desire to shame and blame. However, conflict, when used properly, can be a powerful source of healing. The process of resolution meets compassion.

I think of my two daughters with arms so heavy they can't reach out. The work that lies ahead requires strength and perseverance. A commitment made to be fit enough to tackle all the difficult obstacles we need to clear.

Emotional conflict can become an event with a dialogue. Feelings become facts, and we might base our reality on who was there when the pain began. My daughters see me as a mother who was not their protector, and never showed up when needed most. I stand accused. And all the while I hold steadfast to my truth. I won't give away my power by allowing others to define who I am: A good, kind, and loving mother, grandmother, wife, and friend. Whatever my character defects, I have forgiven myself for yesterday. Onward, as I push forward, looking back, only to see how far I have come.

When the Implication Is Your Wrong Doing

(Ariella Neville Photo)

I BECAME THE mother I wish I had. This took an extraordinary amount of emotional work. At one time, my daughters were humbled by my history. They admired my ability to walk this earth in kindness while the wounded child lived within. They were proud to be my children. But today it's all so different. My strengths and weaknesses are all seen as character flaws.

When we try to have a relationship with someone

who has not resolved their past, it creates an unsettled future. Blame is used as a means of releasing the pain. As long as this persists, there is no potential to heal. The epiphany shines when the realization takes hold. No one has the power to make us feel emotionally conflicted. This does become a choice. Though they might help, apologies won't soothe the memory of a painful experience. This is work and takes due diligence to bring peace to all things troubling.

My parents were completely inept at raising a child. But there are no do-overs. Coming to terms with the reality that they truly did their best was my path to forgiveness. Nobody wakes up in the morning saying, "Hello, new day, I can't wait to F**K this whole thing up." Adopting a belief that anyone can do better than their best is waiting for the cat to bark.

My memories have no potential to be rewritten. I can't un-remember the fear caused by my mother chasing her demons. This has become part of who I am, and a humbling tale of survival.

As children, we are victims of our circumstances. As adults, we have a responsibility to process our past. We can use our pain to create a purpose and proceed in kindness. OR we can use our pain to create more.

Be better, not bitter.

Thanksgiving

(Christine Parsons Photo)

SEVERAL YEARS AGO, I went to NYC to visit my daughter. My eldest asked to join, and it was the first time the three of us were alone together as adults. I thought it would be filled with an elevation of emotion and gratitude for the way our lives had evolved us to this moment. Divorces, remarriages, and an addition of a bonus baby. Yes, sometimes riddled in turmoil. But here we were. All three of us girls, all grown up.

The visit turned out to have a constant undertow. It felt like a riptide that lashed around our ankles, with a force of unearthing past trauma. We were so, obviously, unresolved, and the elephant was beckoning estrangement. A myriad of unsettling innuendoes found me walking on eggshells.

Our conversations led to remembrances of past holidays. The chaos of blended family. That sense of fearful dual loyalty. Always one parent whose feelings created doubt. Who to choose without stirring up anger? But this year, the father and wife were traveling for Thanksgiving. In the wake of his proposed absence, one daughter shared that she was coming home for her high school reunion. My other daughter lives two hours away. What a glorious plan we hatched that day. My family would be together with no strings attached. No doubt or worry of sensitive feelings. I arrived home with this news. My husband and I each grew in our excitement. Family gatherings were becoming few and far between.

As October turned the page on the calendar to November, I made the first call to my eldest, Zoey (two hours away). "Do you think you will come Wednesday before Thanksgiving? Or drive-up Thursday morning?" Thinking I was going to hear a soft-spoken response, I could not have prepared myself for anger. "Why does Thanksgiving always have to be about you? I'm married now and this year is my in-law's turn to have us for the holiday."

I began to stutter and defend my truth, "But what about our discussion at Tiegan's? I thought we planned to spend Thanksgiving together this year?" More chaos. "What are you talking about? There is no way I would have agreed to that!" And I held steadfast to my reality. When I hung up, I looked at my husband and asked, "When I got back from NY, didn't I say that we had made plans for all of us to be together?" I knew he would confirm, but it did not release me of those initial feelings of insanity.

So, while I was already in despair, I thought, "Why not? Just rip off the Band-Aid." And I called my other daughter. More anger. "What are you talking about?! Why would I come all that way? We don't even have a car!" More stuttering...and the conversation ended with the implication of my crazy.

I spent the next couple of weeks wrapping my brain around what Thanksgiving was going to look like. Our son was living in Colorado, and I had spent time trying to figure out airplane flights. This is a time when air travel is hideously expensive. But I was determined to have my family together. This recent turn of events, found my plans dissolved. The holiday would be spent in different states. My husband and I were invited to our neighbor's house, and we accepted.

As we were heading out the door, the afternoon of Thanksgiving, the phone rang. My instinct and the angel on my shoulder shrieked in a high-pitched voice, "Don't answer it!" My younger daughter's name was vivid on the Caller ID. But the devil on my other shoulder was quite persistent and sneered, "What could it hurt?" Oh my...it could hurt a lot.

Once again, thinking what I was going to hear, was not even close. The perplexity of dual loyalty announced in such a way it could not be ignored.

"Hi Mom, happy Thanksgiving."

"Hi Tiegan, happy Thanksgiving to you. Where are you guys spending the day?"

"Oh, we're in the car with Dad and Alice (stepmom) headed to Zoey's."

Cue the sound of my heart barely beating as every breath became an effort

Ignorance would have been such a happy place. And I felt the crushing blow of unsolicited information. My family was spending the day together without me.

I remember the instant nausea. The room spinning, and the effort it took to not scream. It was a death that I felt. I clutched at the wall for support with phone still in hand. Somehow, I remained standing. It took every ounce of my will power to shave off the hard edges of the voice inside of me. I vaguely recall expressing the time on the clock, and how we needed to get to our neighbors. I wished her a pleasant day, and fell to my knees as I hung up the phone.

I laid there in my pool of tears. Hard as I tried, I was incapable of reining it in. The pain took my whole body with wracking sobs. All pride was gone as fluids poured out of my eyes and nose. Oh, it was an ugly cry. My dear sweet husband held me as he gently validated my gut-wrenching emotions, "I am so sorry. This must hurt so much."

As another Thanksgiving approaches, I remember that girl lying on the floor. This is the time of year when you will hear with frequency, "Family is everything." But this is true only if you are everything to family. There is a weird notion of DNA and how we define what our relationships should be. The truth is, everyone has stuff. Everyone. Our propensity is to be that Hallmark movie or a Norman Rockwell painting that exemplifies unity. But we are human, and no one is perfect. If we see ourselves as broken china, we can be put back together with strands of gold. When we see our cracks and crevices, it is with a vision of being so beautifully flawed.

I have learned that family is not about blood. Family are the people who will hold your hand when you need it most. Yes, sometimes my mind strays to a conjured-up image of my daughters, their spouses and children gathered around my table. But then I take myself back to that visit in NY, and the estrangement elephant begging us to revisit painful chapters. There really is no way to pretend that bad things never happened. How we resolve our own emotional conflict is the difference between clarity and confusion.

Be you, and replace fear with love. Happy Thanksgiving and peace to your tender heart.

Choices

(Christine Parsons Photo)

Dear Zoey and Tiegan,

Being an estranged mother, is a very "strange" place to live. It is knowing that we have reached irreconcilable differences without effort to reconcile. Silence guarantees that this will never get better.

I have been told that I need to change. But what does that mean? I stopped being the person I was yesterday, and all the days before. The power of my knowledge is gaining with every breath I take.

I made a decision a few years ago. My fall down the rabbit hole provoked a need to stay alive. The best way for me to do this, is to write. It is my greatest gift, and gives me the grace to override the horrific feelings of isolation. I openly share the emotions of despair. It's like being in cement shoes, because it seems impossible to move us forward. There are days when my reality finds me on the other side of a locked door that has no key. So many emotional memories of being told my best was never good enough. My efforts to be better were met with, "We will never forgive you." And, "This is not fixable." So, what are my choices? The only thing that makes sense is to believe you. Waiting for never is a long time.

Estranged parents approach each day with grief. "Morning means Mourning." Grieving for loved ones who are still alive. Parents who try to imagine what the adult child is thinking. Who have they become? And for those of us who are grandparents, the pain of missing all the milestones matches a visual of dishes being shattered on a cement floor. A continual reel that plays, "Will we ever move away from this horrible space?" And the word, "never" resounds. In the interim, our lives go on, and so we must live.

My writing isn't shared with the intention to shame you. The truth is, I understand the choices you are making and why. Everything you have said to me has meaning. I have learned to read between the lines. An expression of emotions so great that the hurt must be divided. I feel your pain. And I am so sorry that all of this seems a mountain too high to climb. The process of arriving at a solution has been to remain perfectly still. This makes sense to me. My ongoing pursuit, as being a student of human behavior, has enriched me with compassion.

We all make decisions based on where we place the most value. While I love you so dearly, your love feels unattainable to me right now. And so, I make my choices based on that. I, therefore, speak to all the estranged parents who also love deeply. They, too, are on this quest to stay alive. We are all in a struggle of recognizing how much we hate the behavior and not the people. When I hear, "This is not fixable," I stay mindful of how fixable it really is. It is to use our words as a tool to put back together all the things that appear to be irreparably broken.

"A life lived without regret is a life filled with purpose." How many times have I said this? Too many times to count. If I sit in a place of second-guessing my life, I rob myself of what is yet to come. Constantly living in yesterday is a fruitless pursuit. I must stay present within my own reality. Today, I am an estranged mother, and an alienated grandmother. All my decisions are based on that truth. And while the road ahead seems endless…I know there is a place where we can arrive.

Our past dialogues are mentioned in commemoration of all the things that beg to be healed. My hope springs eternal in the face of "never." My arms remain wide open for as long as it takes to envelope you. My lap, though small, is big enough to cradle you. When your mind says that I stopped loving you, your heart speaks the truth. My hope is that you continue to find comfort in knowing that I am right here, where I have always been.

Love,
Mom

Holidaze

(Christine Parsons Photo)

IT'S THAT TIME of year when every estranged parent imagines all the ways to finally make things right. Money, gifts, texts, e-mails, or maybe even showing up unannounced. The fear of making things worse is paralyzing. And, for a lot of us, we have crawled into a corner with great effort to be as quiet as a mouse.

For me, the nightmare of trying to make things better found me whirling as I circled the drain. Hearing the responses of silence, or more character defects left me with a sense of being completely powerless. I lived in a world of implication that I have ruined lives. But then I had to ask myself, "When was I given this much power?"

I see this journey of estrangement as living the worst of what can happen. My fear of being public with my thoughts, and sharing this experience has dissipated. Nothing I do makes these circumstances any better. Connecting with others who share this journey has created a community. Instead of the horrific feelings of shame and isolation, I feel surrounded by acceptance for who I am.

I asked my son, "Do you think writing a book and being out loud about estrangement is OK? Am I making things worse?" His response, "You are doing everything you need in order to cope. Your writing helps others."

And this has become the advice I give others. Find a constructive mechanism that will help you cope, and create something positive. Commit to Self-Care. My experience has taught me a hard truth. My acts of kindness are received as an ongoing attempt to deconstruct something that took great effort to build. It takes a long time to form a belief. Once there, it is met with an unwillingness to believe an alternative. Think of it as a free fall into uncertainty. We come to rely on what believe to be true.

I have stopped my efforts to facilitate healing. Every once in a while, I will send a text or an e-mail. But this is done to soothe my own heart. I do this without expectation of a response. I have blocked all extended families on social media. Being privy to lives gone on without me is like watching a fatal car crash over and over again. I have put trust in my own belief that when my children are ready to heal, they will reach out. We will begin a dialogue meant to move us forward.

I pray you make time in the coming weeks to nourish your soul. Gather your posse and circle the wagons. Try to change a tradition to create something new. The picture shown above is my fake tree that is not trying to pretend it is anything else. It comforts me because it doesn't represent any past memories. It keeps me on my forward march and living in today.

Peace to your tender hearts.

Letters of Amends?

(Ariella Neville Photo)

WHEN I READ articles that suggest I haven't listened responsibly, apologized correctly, or owned my wrongdoing, I feel completely defeated. The nature of estrangement places blame on one person. Naming character defects, followed by complete silence, holds us to a blank page. We understand there is pain, but where are its roots?

The only apology received is the one that is heard. For most of us we have cried, begged, pleaded and, incoherently babbled words that might move us away from the threatened silence. We have cried tears with snot running from every orifice, as the terror of this reality begs for it stop. Tragically, once the adult child makes the decision that there is nothing you can say to make it right, it will stay wrong. The accusations become the arsenal. The silence becomes a weapon of mass destruction as the damage spreads.

At first, the bereft parent shoulders the burden. "If it wasn't for me, my family would be OK. I am a horrible human being." Eventually time gives way to the ripple effect. Everywhere we look the estrangement is seeping into every corner of the house. Once each room is filled with the chaos, the ripple effect begins to seep into the community. So many souls have become involved. I have yet to find one person who celebrates my fragmented family.

When you know all your attempts are seen as wrongdoing, the burden on your shoulders might become lighter. Slowly you will come to terms with the realization that, no matter how hard you try, you can't do anything right. A letter of amends becomes an effort of grasping at straws. What are we really apologizing for? The only way to clearly accept your own wrong doing is to sit with the person who feels the conflict. That discussion will lead to the alternative of what to do the next time troubling emotions rise. Because now we know that estrangement just makes everything so much worse.

The silence demands that we fall prey to hearsay and conjecture. The truth becomes blurred. Like the game of Telephone, information reaches us after it has passed through many hands. Magical thinking takes over and we ruminate on things that might not be true.

My advice to anyone who experiences conflict without opportunity for a conversation: Work through your own anger. Free yourself of expectation. Reconciliation requires us to be calm and collectively accountable.

Writing a letter of amends does have its value, but only if it's reciprocated. Each one of us has participated in wrongdoing. All these knee-jerk reactions have bruised us from head to toe. Yes, our children are hurting, and so are we. The reality of amends is an admission, from all those who share the relationship, to be completely open and honest. We didn't arrive her by ourselves, and the perceived failure is not one-sided.

Peaceful minds want things to get better. A mind embroiled in chaos, can't see healthy solutions. As much as I tried to take this all on my shoulders, I collapsed from the weight. Picking myself up off the ground required me to understand that this is not about "muscling" through. I have evolved my thinking about being strong. It has nothing to do with my physical body. It is the willingness to be brave inside my heart and my mind.

Past trauma is soothed when the dialogue names the events that created the perceived harm. If we can stop asking, "Who happened?" we might get to the root of the problem by asking, "What happened?"

Being an estranged parent finds us with a sense of foreboding of what comes next. I pray that you find the courage that will give you strength to live this life fully. Continue to speak your truth. This is not your fault. You are here with a purpose.

If My Daughters Were Listening

(Ariella Neville Photo)

ESTRANGED PARENTS OFTEN wonder if their spoken word has ever resonated in the heart of their child. If any action was considered as a declaration of unconditional love. If the ongoing reality of doing the best we can with what we know is realized. If the strides we take for tomorrow were seen. If they understand that we are all in constant transition of the people we are yet to become.

If my daughters were listening, I would tell them

that I had to save my life. It was necessary to turn my unrelenting pain into something worthwhile. I found it necessary to emotionally write in order to relieve my own heart. This path can bring us to a deprecating sense of isolation. The offering of my experiences has found a community of other mothers and fathers. A collection of souls who have thoughts and feelings of desperation, shame, and loneliness. I wish to lend a hand to other grandparents by pulling them back into the light. My work has become a celebration of the life I have been given.

If my daughters were listening, I would tell them that I keep hope eternal. It will never be too late. That I long to write the chapter of how we heal our past. I have a vision of our energy pushing us forward and out of this space. Leaving behind all the things that have already happened through the process of learning why they happened. I want to share the work of commitment that evolves us into goodness. How our choice of words is in great effort to be productive. The miracle of conversations that finally give way to compassion and understanding.

If my daughters were listening, I would tell them that I love deeply. I no longer wish for days gone by. Though our mother-daughter relationships once flourished, there was an undertow that was pulling us into darkness. As many of our past chapters beg to be revisited, they can serve only as a means to be better in right now. It is easy to fall into bitterness, but this proves only to be a mindset of self-harm. The alternative is to be brave. Shine light. Accept what is…until the imminent evolution of change.

If my daughters were listening, I would repeat, "I love you. I want you in my life. What do I need to do to move us to a better place?"

If my daughters were listening, I would tell them I am right here where I have always been.

When Left Unspoken

(Ariella Neville Photo)

AS A VERBAL processor, I have an incessant need to talk things through. Oh, this journey of being silenced is undeniably my greatest challenge. I stand accused at the hand of the other parent: "You always have to talk about feelings. You just can't let anything go. The girls don't want to hear this S**T!!" Well, maybe nobody wants to hear me, but I know all things that need to be said are a necessary means to an end. Without a discussion, the unsettling emotions will prevail.

Our estrangement is born of a past consumed with mental turmoil. Since I was there at the time of the conflict, I have become the source. But blaming me has not made anything better. It has just become a foregone conclusion. There is no line of defense when the truth is blurred.

Years ago, I read a book called How to Talk So Your Kids Will Listen, and How to Listen So Your Kids Will Talk. It was my bible for many years. I tried, in earnest, to be open to everything I might be urged to discuss and what I might hear. When my (then) sixteen-year-old daughter called to tell me, a large group was camping in somebody's field, I immediately felt the weight of my decision yet to be made. I had never heard of the boy who initiated the invitation, and I knew it was a gathering created with the mindset to party. And yet, responsibly, these teenagers were creating an environment to cut loose where no one would attempt to drive. I remember saying, "Yes, OK." And followed with an urging: "I hope someday when you have a teenage daughter, and she calls for this same type of permission, you will remember this moment, and how hard it must have been for me to say yes." Once my girls were in high school, I fought the inclination of wanting to micromanage their lives. I stayed conscious of the reality that I was raising adults. Tender minds that needed to become critical thinkers, by developing their own power of reasoning. Problem solving is an acquired skill.

I told all three of my children during their teen

years, "My hope is that someday, when I am not with you, you will hear the sound of my voice." In other words, I prayed that every iota of advice, guidance, and heartfelt wishes would resound in my absence. Now, I am left to wonder. What stuck? Or is everything a point of conflict and rebuttal? Was all of my motherly intention lost in this muck and mire of leftover crap?

Estrangement. The gripping fears that follow in its wake. Everything left unspoken and unresolved has the potential to be forever. When my own mother died, it became the sound of a slamming door. Our relationship was riddled with ambivalence. We were constantly entrenched in opposing thoughts and feelings. At age twenty-two, I had little knowledge of how death was a finality that would affect me for the rest of my life.

When I saw the movie Terms of Endearment, soon after my mother's passing, I was unprepared. It felt like a stake to my heart when Aurora (the mother) screamed as she watched her daughter take her last breath, "I'm so stupid, so stupid. Somehow, I thought, somehow, I thought when she finally went that...that it would be a relief. Oh, my sweet little darling. Oh dear, there's nothing harder! THERE'S NOTHING HARDER!" It was everything I felt and wanted to scream.

My mother and I never had the opportunity to have an adult relationship. But I often wonder what conversations we might have had, given the chance.

And I think of my daughters in this regard, as I pray that someday will be today. Ceasing the moment that will reveal how our differences are reconcilable. It will never be too late, until it's too late.

The Value of a Sincere Apology

(Ariella Neville Photo)

MY SON WAS working a job last summer. One of his new hires had a visceral reaction to a song that was playing on Spotify. The man quietly pleaded, "Can you please change this? It's attached to a really bad experience, and it's kinda freakin me out." My son responded immediately, "I'm so sorry." And he changed the station without question.

When we offer kindness in a sincere apology, we bestow the power of empathy. We don't always have to understand why someone is hurting. The ability to react with compassion validates that there is the presence of a cause. This immediately soothes the nervous system when we know we are being heard.

The contrary experience is to place blame. To imply that the other person is not of sound mind. Taking it further by shaming them for having an emotional response. As an estranged mother, I was constantly cast as being irrational because of a perceived mental instability. This has become a huge trigger when anyone attempts to belittle my state of wellbeing.

Shame and blame immediately break trust. How can you ever be certain of another person when you know they don't have your best interest at heart? It is difficult, at best, to go back to the way it was. When someone reacts to your feelings with, "What's wrong with you?" For me, a door immediately slams shut.

The opposite experience is when someone realizes your emotional reaction is based out of fear. "What happened to you?" This is a powerful way of offering another person sensitivity and consideration. When you are aware that your emotions are under suspicion, you will be in a constant state of second guessing yourself.

Our human relationships become quite fragile when conflict rises. It is the way we reconcile that will create the stepping stones to how we proceed. When we are brave, we are easily accountable. Facing adversity from a place of strength.

Getting What You Deserve?

(Ariella Neville Photo)

AFTER TWO YEARS of estrangement from my daughters, I went to talk to the father. I admit, it was my version of insanity. With decades of knowledge of how he motivates, I have lost the right to be surprised. Expecting kindness or assistance is my ongoing journey of waiting for the cat to bark. For over thirty years, it's been a constant battle of wits. Psychological warfare that requires me to survive with the least amount of bloodshed.

No matter what angle I took, to operate within the best interest of our daughters, it was a sole effort.

My belief in human goodness kept me vigilant, and I continuously offered us a new beginning. This was all due to my own deafness. I admit to ignoring all of his attempts of telling me exactly how limited our relationship truly was. Therefore, my expectation of compassion was like trying to draw water from an empty well.

So, there I was. Driving the short distance across town with my heart in my throat. It was upon entry into his home, the first words he spoke: "I am not going to help you. I don't care about you. And I don't want to be your friend."

What followed was a litany of parroted dialogue. It was all too familiar. The accusations were almost in verbatim to what I had already heard as my character defects. His wife came down the stairs, and they verbally accosted me in stereo. "You need to stop being so jealous of us. We don't blame the girls for not wanting you around their children. Nobody ever knows when you are going to snap. You just don't act right. Maybe you should read some books. You ruin every family gathering." This is when I realized the collective attempt to brain wash me into believing their truth.

There was a time when I adopted that I was beyond redemption. Too many people were reiterating my deep and penetrating flaws. The repeated dialogue bulleted me in their consensus. I was a horrible mother. Filled with anger and rage. Never acting in the best interest of my children. Using them as pawns for my own personal gain. Not being there when they needed me most. And yet, I became keenly aware that everything can't be my fault.

Their memories were not aligning with my truth. Did I get mad and lose my temper? Did I say things I wish I could take back? Did my instincts fail me at times? Is there a moment that I wish for a do over? Yes, to all the above. It's a funny thing about being human. Our lives are not always filled with moments of brilliance.

Am I getting what I deserve? Well, every indicator seems to point to that…until my truth breaks free. This guilt is a prison of my own design.

I remember telling another person about the accusations of failure. I revealed that my motherhood was scrutinized under a microscope. I shared the pervasive need of my family to expose every ugly crack and crevice. The woman asked, "Do you believe you're a failure?" I remember stuttering, "No." In that moment I understood that I was faltering by the implied suggestions. This, despite the fact that there was no real evidence of my wrongdoing. The question I had to ask myself, "Will you allow others to define who you are?"

It was then that I took back my life. Unfettered by discerning eyes, I was free of the guilt. No more shame. I realized that I had given away my power by allowing others to tell me what I think, how I feel, and the way I treat people.

Repeat after me: I am a good, kind, loving parent, partner, friend, and grandmother/grandfather.

This is not your fault. You are not choosing to perpetuate the pain. When we can accept that our challenges are meant to be our teacher, purpose evolves. The ability to really see simplicity gives us sight to all the constant tiny miracles. Don't wait for moments of grandeur, for they are few and far between.

Peace to all who walk this path.

Would You Do It Again?

(Christine Parsons Family Album)

IN 2004, I believed I had never known a pain greater than being estranged from my own child. I had no idea what I was going to be required to survive. Today, there has been a collection of years that find me estranged for the third time. This time the pain is exacerbated because now I am a grandmother.

There was a short time when I was given opportunity to transition into this glorious role as GG. Being Gorgeous Grandma was a feeling of unweighted freedom. My heart lifted through their tender hugs and I cherished the moments when they gently patted my face with their chubby hands. And then, suddenly without warning, it would appear that I had vanished into thin air. "Where did I go?" This question haunts me with all the potential answers.

My first year of estrangement as a grandmother is reflected upon as an instinct to survive. Every day was met with the magnitude of the most gut-wrenching emotions. I couldn't sleep, nor could I eat. I spent a year of running to the bathroom as my stomach could never quite settle. My thoughts were like boulders. Too heavy to move my mind away from these babes who must wonder, "Where is Pop and GG?" My own brain literally plagued me. And I wanted to die. My heart hurt so severely at times I couldn't breathe. And I still wake up crying, all these years later. Morning means mourning.

There are many psychologists who write books and articles on, "How to Reconcile." They are written with all the dos and don'ts of what to say and how to act. This puts so much pressure on the parent who believes this is theirs to fix. Passer's by are quite certain that you probably said or did something that provoked these horrible consequences. The suggestions leave little room for the necessary truth.

Reconciliation, most assuredly, requires a round table discussion. It is a gathering of all parties meeting face to face. Coming together with a willingness to be accountable. Getting real with the role we played in all the things that went wrong. My question to the experts is: "Can you have a productive argument by yourself?" Because the answer given in silence seems clear. You can't mend a broken relationship by yourself no matter how impeccable you are in your word. If the other person is not ready to engage in the process, the work that lies ahead can only be your own.

So, I write. Sharing my own stories of how real this s**t gets. The ripple effect of a lone decision. A short-term solution that creates deep and penetrating long-term effects. The complications of estrangement do not just hurt the person intended. It's like a tornado that twisters through a whole community of people who care about you and your family. I have yet to meet one person who delights in my grief and sense of loss. My posse grieves with me.

My first book is called, My Parents are Dead, But I Still Wish They'd Change. Thus, allowing in my sense of humor. My childhood was spent watching my parents chase their demons. As a teenager, my anger and resentment fueled my purpose. My mission? I would make them pay by mixing dangerous cocktails of drugs and alcohol. A weird belief that my own demise would make them suffer. My "aha moment came when I stood at the edge of a cliff, standing on rocks that were giving way beneath my feet. If I didn't jump back to solid ground, my future would be short lived. I was in full comprehension that resentment is the bitter pill you swallow while waiting for others to fall.

My life is a mixture of pain, doubt, brilliance,

failure, triumph, beauty, ugliness, joy, and despair. The minute I decided to be part of my whole story, I released doubt. Too often we focus on specific moments, as we share the chapters that hold all the highlights while standing outside painful experiences. We hesitate to give respect to the darkness. I have found, in my experience, that the knowing of despair gifts me with the brilliance of joy.

Tell your whole story. Be proud of who you are. Continue to be live and not just be alive. My mantra: Use your pain and find a purpose. Gain a sense of direction and proceed in kindness. The only alternative is to use pain to create more of the same.

I do wonder if my daughters could go back, would they change their fateful decision? Would they choose estrangement? Pause in knowing the ripple effect? The sadness of including the grandchildren? The consequence of struggles that now look insurmountable? Would they be more eager to communicate? Would they do anything to avoid telling complicated stories just to divert the truth?

My husband, son, and I have love that grows deeper. We bumble and we fall while continuing to tell the realities of how we got up, no matter how ugly. We are beautifully flawed souls who keep gaining emotional intelligence through the wisdom of today that will create a better tomorrow.

In the meantime, where did I go?

Epilogue

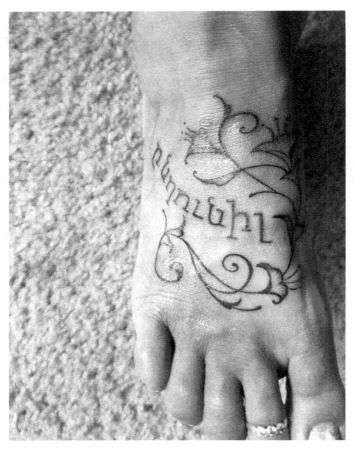

(Christine Parsons Photo)

I HAD THIS tattoo etched into my foot as a constant reminder to allow. It is written in Armenian, which is a significant part of my DNA. I live my life in accordance of this definition: to receive, to accept, to admit, to adopt, to agree.

If only I was aware that there was a dark cloud looming over my family. But I only knew what I knew at the time, and now I know more. Looking through a lens of hindsight only creates sadness over all the things I cannot change. I am better when my feet are planted in right now.

When I do turn around, I can see all the little bread crumbs being dropped. The tiny innuendos that I was constantly misbehaving and falling short of expectations. I was given a goal post that I could never reach. I told my daughters once, "You could give me a script to read, and I would still get it wrong." Oh, that horrible feeling that your best was never good enough.

I am careful about missing my family because I must remember what I'm missing. I understand, now, that our family relationships were not so great. I built on a belief that I could love my daughters through their hardships. As time passes, we tend to remember the best of who we were by putting the worst up on a shelf. I accept that every spoken word is forever. I keep my balance by acknowledging my story as a whole.

I work on the trauma of this experience by allowing it in. It is to create a mindset that this chapter does not define my entire existence. I do admit, for a while, my identity was all about being an estranged parent, alienated from her grandchildren. It was a good and proper suffering. And because I believed it was all my fault, I deserved every bit of the pain.

But this is a space where I dare not dwell. My husband reminds me of abundance. I am given the grace of inner strength in knowing that I am a work in progress. Compassion received is compassion that I gift to others.

I refer to family as chosen. We are a collection of DNA and non-DNA souls who can see each other without judgement. I am empowered by those who applaud me at my best, and tenderly forgive me for my worst. If the self-deprecating dialogue starts ringing in my head, I look at the weather, and call the person who will drive through a storm. I am humbled to walk this path with my dignity intact.

When we understand there are circumstances where we cannot impose our will, we free ourselves of all the things that are not ours to own. What other people do and say is none of our business. "Sweep the ground in front of your own door." ~German Proverb~

Remember to flip the dialogue when you're tempted to blurt out, "What's wrong with you?" The better alternative: "What happened to you?" Give other people the gift of having their feelings, even when you don't understand the depth of their emotions. Let them know you have compassion when they are triggered by a past experience. If the reaction is greater than the circumstances, chances are, there is more to what you see. When trauma goes unresolved, it becomes behavior that rules every decision.

It is work to free ourselves of anger and resentment. Don't get me wrong, I have raged, cried, and blamed. But I find that when I bring myself to a more peaceful space, my interactions are predominantly led with kindness. I approach conflict with a better sense of calm. When I trust every decision, I free myself from the fear of failure. Life has a guarantee that all things will change.

We are best when we meet people where they are. It is possible to do this without having an expectation that they should be further along. We all make choices based on where we place the most value. Our values evolve as we gain emotional intelligence. Allow….

CPSIA information can be obtained
at www.ICGtesting.com
Printed in the USA
LVHW080222160723
752414LV00007B/412